AF241294

CONVERSATIONS WITH MONEY

A Love Story

HOW TO LOVE YOUR MONEY
AND IT LOVE YOU BACK

Lynda Moore

Copyright © Lynda Moore | Money Mentalist 2022

All rights reserved. No part of this publication may be reproduced, distributed, or transmitted in any form or by any means, including photocopying, recording, or other electronic, or mechanical methods, without the prior written permission of the author or publisher, except in the case of brief quotations embodied in reviews and certain other non-commercial uses permitted by copyright law.

This publication is designed to provide accurate and authoritative information regarding the subject matter covered. It is sold with the understanding that the author or publisher is not engaged in rendering legal, accounting, or other professional services. If legal advice or other expert assistance is required, the services of a competent professional person should be sought.

ISBN: 978-1-99-118530-3

Printed in Australia and the United States of America

YOUR FREE GIFT!

To get the most valuable experience and create your own love story with your money, download the *Money: A Love Story Workbook*. Work through this as you read the book to develop your own money love story, remove financial blocks and create more wealth in your life.

You can get your exclusive copy here:
www.moneymentalist.com/bookbonus

TABLE OF CONTENTS

INTRODUCTION

Some days are etched in our memories forever. It might be your wedding day, the birth of a child or those days that years later you realise were pivotal in the direction that your life would take from that day forward.

It feels like it was only yesterday, but it was over fifteen years ago. It was my birthday (an easy day to remember). It was also the day that my daughter (then aged 17) was heading off to Argentina for a year on a rotary exchange. She was so excited as this trip had been planned and anticipated for quite a long time. I was excited for her as well, but I also knew I would miss her dreadfully; she was my only child, so the empty nest was happening a little earlier than I had anticipated.

I took her to the airport where a group of friends had gathered to wish her farewell. I'm not the greatest of travelers at the best of times; I worry about missing my flight, being late for check-in, and of course, have I got my passport? So, I was all the more anxious for her without having to say farewell too.

Finally, after a lot of farewells and hugs from her friends, it was my turn. We hugged. Then she disappeared through passport control with a cheery wave and was gone.

To cheer me up, a group of friends had organised a birthday dinner for me, so off we went to a local restaurant. We laughed, chatted, ate and drank—it was a fun and successful distraction.

I arrived home to a darkened house. I switched on the lights and looked around my lovely home. It wasn't a large or ostentatious house. The setting made it special, nestled down a long driveway, with native bush as the backdrop and a deck to enjoy in the summer months by the pool. It was the first home I had outside of the city, and although I knew nothing about farming, I loved living in the rural landscape.

This particular evening, it wasn't quite so lovely. I looked around at the house that was no longer my home. The furniture was stacked and ready for the removal company. There were boxes with red stickers for me and blue stickers for him. This was also no longer 'our' home. Our marriage was over, and we were going our separate ways.

I walked outside and sat on a chair on the deck. I looked at the sky. It was a beautiful clear evening; the stars were shining in all their glory. The tears started to flow. The realisation hit—I was alone, my daughter was starting her adventure overseas, my husband had moved out, the house was sold, and our possessions were packed and ready to be moved.

This was not where I thought I would be at this stage of my life. This is not how I wanted to spend my birthday. How had I gotten to this point in my life? What had gone so wrong?

I sat outside for a very long time until there were no more tears left to shed, and wearily I headed back inside to bed.

I know this is not an unusual story, a lot of relationships break up. Marriages fail, we fall out of love, or they just don't work for whatever reason. We grieve and then pick ourselves up and move on. Which is exactly what I did.

So, why am I sharing my story with you? What makes me so different from everyone else whose relationship has ended?

Well, this wasn't my first marriage to end, it was my fourth... and I held a secret that no one knew—I was $600,000 in debt!

Although I didn't realise it at the time, this was the day that the Money Mentalist was conceived.

My journey had begun. Over the next 10 years I studied, I soaked up all the information I could, and I put into practice everything that I teach my clients and will now share with you.

Fast forward to twelve and a half years after that horrible birthday, I received a phone call out of the blue to say my fourth ex-husband, Gaz, was terminally ill with cancer and was in hospice. They just wanted me to know and it was up to me to decide what to do with that information.

I contacted him and for the next month, I was by his side until he passed away quietly in my arms. We were blessed to have that time together to talk about our relationship, how we screwed it up, what really happened, and to forgive each other. The conversations we had during that month were profound, deep, and insightful. One thing we both realised was just how much our inability to communicate effectively about money contributed to our marriage ending. We will never know if our relationship could have been saved if we had known then what we talked about during that month. I made a promise to Gaz that as the Money Mentalist I would make it my mission and the rest of my life's work to help as many couples as I possibly could to not end up as we did. This would be his legacy.

You may think that this is just another book about money, but it's more than that. This is a book about relationships. Your relationship with money. Your partner's relationship with money. And your relationship with each other and money. It's also about love.

You will get to know me and some of my clients as I share our stories so that you can learn as you read, do the exercises, and reflect. There will be laughter, and maybe some tears, but by the end of the book, I hope you will have gained insight and applied the lessons to your own life.

And most of all, it won't take you 10 years to get there.

As you read a chapter, you will find exercises popping up. Grab a journal and write down the answers to those exercises off the top of your head. Then keep reading.

Part three is where you get to deep dive, do the work, and delve deeper into the answers you journaled. If you want to jump to part three, of course, you can but, make sure to give yourself time to absorb the concepts. Working on your relationship with money may be new to you and takes time to soak in.

For the bonus workbook and exclusive readers free gifts please head to www.moneymentalist.com/bookbonus

PART ONE

GETTING TO KNOW YOUR MONEY

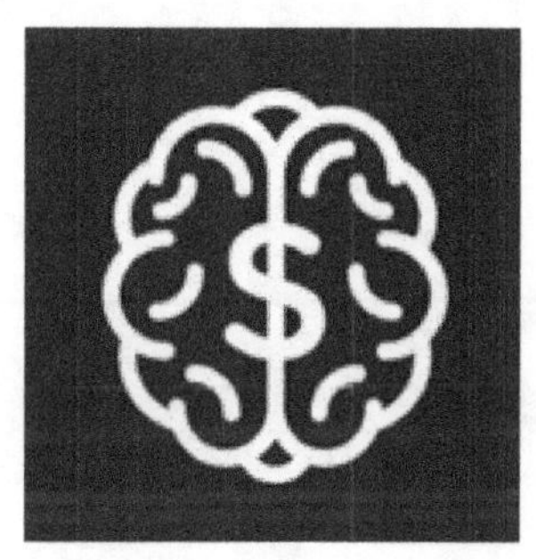

CHAPTER 1

HOW'S YOUR RELATIONSHIP WITH MONEY RIGHT NOW?

Gaz and I were married on our Lifestyle property.

The celebrations went on over a couple of days. Bands and musicians played over the two days to honour our love of music. We owned a café, so there was no shortage of food either. It was magical.

So when did it start to falter? When did the stresses kick in and how did we let the magic slip away?

As with many relationships, there was no one big defining moment, just lots of small things that started to add up. Financial stress was mounting for us. Gaz's consulting contract didn't go to the next stage so his income stopped. We had landlord problems with the café, so instead of having a business to sell, which would have relieved most of our financial stress, our lease simply got terminated and we ended up with nothing but some furniture! My accounting practice was struggling. It was a perfect storm.

Gaz began to withdraw from me. I could see it happening but didn't know how to deal with it; I had enough of my own stuff to worry about. We stopped communicating and just existed together. We didn't acknowledge or even attempt to talk about our situation. I remember after a really tough patch we bought a puppy and I thought to myself, *We must be okay, we've just bought a puppy.* There was more discussion about the puppy than there was about the state of our relationship.

Then it just broke. Gaz was the one who finally said he didn't want to be married anymore. We went to counseling, Gaz moved into the stables (which we had converted into guest accommodation), but by then both of us were so stuck in our own problems–mine financial, his stress and depression–that we didn't know how to pull it back, and despite the fact that we still loved each other, we decided to separate.

Our beautiful home was sold, and we went our separate ways–both of us were heartbroken and devastated, unbeknown to each other at that time.

During his time in hospice, I worked beside him. I told him about my work as Money Mentalist and he asked me lots of questions. Why was I doing this and not my accounting practice? This led to the first time we ever talked about what had happened financially in our relationship, 12 years after the fact.

I told him about how the practice had struggled. He looked at me with surprise. 'I thought the practice was doing well', he said.

'No, it wasn't', I answered.

His eyes widened and his voice got stronger. 'You never told me.'

'No', I replied, 'I didn't. You had enough going on with your own business and I didn't want to add to your stress".

'You never told me; I could have helped. Maybe not financially but I could have helped *you*'.

Those words hit me hard. It had never occurred to me that he could have helped. It never occurred to me how keeping my struggle from him was causing me stress which was causing *him* stress anyway, the very thing I was avoiding. It never occurred to me that not sharing meant we never changed our lifestyle or spending behaviour or did anything different. Me not saying anything got us further into debt and further apart.

He acknowledged struggles he'd withheld too. In our attempt to protect the other from additional stresses, we actually added to them. Who knows if our marriage would have remained intact if we'd done the work I now do with clients and will share with you in this chapter and beyond. What if we had helped each other challenge our money beliefs, investigated our money personalities, and aligned our way of living with our individual and shared values and lived within our means?

Our conversations in those last few weeks showed me the importance of communication–talking to each other and sharing everything, not just the easy stuff. That month changed me and the way I think about Money Mentalist. It isn't just a business, it has a lifeblood of its own. It's Gaz's legacy and it drives me to succeed at helping other couples sort out their own money stuff so they can connect more deeply. It drives me to help individuals do their crucial self-work so they can relate to others and money from the healthiest mindset.

You have a chance to do it differently. No matter what age or stage of life you're in, you can improve your relationship with money.

That's right, *you are in a relationship with money.* And that relationship needs tending just like your human relationships.

So let's imagine this for a minute. **If you were dating money, what would it say about you?**

I love this question. I always get a sideways curious look when I ask it. It's not something we tend to think about. We date people, not money.

The first thing we need to understand about money is that whether we like it or not, we have a relationship with it. It's the longest relationship you will ever have. It will outlast friendships, quite possibly your significant other, and family. It was there before you were born as your parents planned your arrival. And it will be there after you are gone when those you leave behind stand beside your coffin wondering how much they will get!

Whilst it's a fun question, it's also an important one. Think about your answer right now. *If you were dating money, what would it say about you?*

Here are a few interesting answers I've heard over the years.

'Money would dump me! I'm a really bad date!'

'I ignored Money, so it got bored with me, and moved on to someone else.'

'I kept money in the dark about my goals and my dreams, so we just lived in the moment and had no love left when we needed it.'

'Money and I partied hard and wore each other out!'

'Money pays me a lot of attention, shows me lots of opportunities, thinks about me a lot and cares if I go away, it will look for me to make sure I come back.'

'Money and I should have been more adventurous.'

'Money feels nurtured and appreciated. It needs to have a bit of freedom to do its own thing and grow, but we also like each other's company.'

'Money wants to pay me more attention and spoil me more than I let it. I'm very protective of my relationship, it's a nurturing relationship.'

'Money and I worked hard to make a brand-new start together. We got to know each other slowly and have grown and matured together.'

'Money wants a bit more space, I smother it and hang on too tightly.'

As you can see from these answers, when we think about it, we can see clearly that we are in a relationship with our money, and having a healthy one is important.

Our relationship with money sets the scene for all our other relationships in life as well. If you are stressed and anxious about your money you will bring that anxiety into your relationships. If you are relaxed and comfortable with your money you will find it easier to talk to your partner about money in a relaxed easy way.

As with any relationship, your relationship with money will change over time.

When we are young and have very little or no financial responsibility, our relationship with money tends to be a bit like that too—we don't need to worry about it and we can try lots of different money dates until we find the one that suits us.

As we grow and take on more responsibility for ourselves and others, we don't want to be serial money daters anymore. It's time to settle down and start to nurture and grow the relationship we have. There will be times when money leaves us, and it is up to us to choose how we want to restart the relationship and on what terms.

You see this is the main difference between dating money and dating a person. Money won't argue, it won't push back, it won't tell you what you can and can't do with it. The choices you make with your money are entirely your choices. Realising that you have made some not-great choices with money and have hurt yourself, as a result, can be a tough pill to swallow. But you can make up again and do things differently if you choose to do so.

Now it's your turn. Pull out your journal and off the top of your head answer this question: If I was dating money what would it say about me?

Your *deep dive* into this question is within the 'Conversations with Money Exercise' in Part three.

What's Your Money Personality?

It's easy to get caught up in personality traits and end up putting ourselves in boxes. When I was studying psychology, I found the "Big 5" personality traits fascinating. I could see myself fitting into each of them at different stages of life, and sometimes I could be all five in one day!

It's the same with our money personality. I am a spender at heart; I love to shop. I love to spend. The price tag doesn't matter; whether it's a box of chocolates for a friend or impulse buying a car (yes, I did do that, more than once!). It's the joy of spending that gives me a buzz.

At times, I've allowed my Spender personality to enable me to justify my behaviour and make it okay. 'What do you expect, I'm a spender,' was my stock standard answer after arriving home with arms full of goodies. It enabled me to continue a pattern of behaviour that kept me deep in debt, and looking back now, no longer served me. Nobody asked me, 'Why are you spending?' If they had I would have been forced to look at my behaviour and start digging into what was going on a lot sooner than I did.

So yes, it is great to know what your money personality is–take it lightly, have fun with it, but don't let it rule your life.

Your 'money personality' is a behavioural pattern relating to your spending and saving. At different times in your life, and depending on circumstances, you may see more than one money personality type in yourself and that's quite natural.

You'll also probably see a cross-over between money personalities as well–in other words, you can show parts of more than one money personality at the same time. There's no good or bad money personality–they all have benefits and downsides.

And the best news is, it doesn't define you for life–you can change it.

These money personalities were developed in the 1980s by Olivia Mellan, a clinical psychologist (now retired) who specialised in relationship and money issues. You can find the quiz on our website www.moneymentalist.com.

Here are the five main money personalities. As you read them, see which one you relate to the most.

Hoarder

Saving money is important to you, as are your financial goals. These are priorities in your life. You enjoy the process of planning and reviewing your budget and you stick to it.

Spending money on luxury items for yourself and your family is difficult. Even purchasing practical gifts can seem wasteful to you.

Spending money on entertainment and holidays is just unnecessary. You may even struggle to buy new clothes when you still have perfectly 'good' things in the wardrobe.

'Saving for a rainy day' is your motto. Long-term security is important, particularly in retirement. You want your money tucked away safely rather than somewhere you can easily access it.

Spender

Instant gratification, immediate pleasure, spend it now and worry about tomorrow later. You enjoy spending your money not only on yourself but on gifts for others as well.

Budget? What budget? I don't need to save; I can use my credit card. Saving for retirement will only happen if you automate the deduction directly from your income, it just isn't a priority right now.

You find it easy to overspend, which results in debt.

(It's important to note that some people in debt aren't over-spenders—they may not earn enough to meet their basic needs. This is a completely different issue.)

Avoider

You have a hard time managing your money. You have a rough idea of how much you earn, but you don't know where it goes, how much you have in your bank accounts, or how much you owe on your credit cards.

Paying your bills and setting up automatic payments to make your life easier is in the too-hard basket!

Like Spenders, you'll do anything to avoid a budget and your financial record keeping is either non-existent or lots of paper shoved in a drawer somewhere.

If you somehow manage to accumulate some spare money, investing it is just too hard, too detailed, and you just won't get around to it.

What fuels this avoidance? You may feel incompetent or overwhelmed when faced with the tasks of your money life.

Monk

A traditional Money Monk believes that 'Money is the root of all evil'. Money is dirty–it's bad. If you have too much of it, you won't be a good person.

You relate to people of modest means rather than with those that you perceive as 'wealthy'.

If a windfall comes your way (Great Aunt Jean leaves you some money in her will, for example), you're going to feel stressed and worried that you might become greedy and selfish, and you'll be concerned that you may lose sight of your ideals and values.

A modern Money Monk has a very strong social conscious when it comes to spending. You want to make sure your products are ethically sourced and produced. Going to the local markets and sourcing natural and organic products is important to you.

Amasser

Money, money, money. The more you have the happier you are. You can choose whether to spend it, save it, or invest it. If you don't have money, you feel hollow and a bit down. Money is important to your self-worth and gives you a feeling of power, so without it, feelings of being a failure and depression can set in.

Control is important to you, so giving up control even to professionals who have your best interest at heart can be difficult for you.

Some Amassers like to be showy and 'flash the cash' around. They can be perceived as being a bit stingy–they either can't see the point in spending or they tell themselves that when they reach a certain target, then they will celebrate.

Money Mastery

(This final category was developed by Dr. Kathleen Gurney.)

The members of this group make wise financial decisions. They enjoy managing their own money, but they also trust their advisors. They're satisfied with what they have achieved financially.

They make logical decisions. They've learned to take time and not let their emotions run away with them. They understand their values and make decisions that fit with those values both financially and personally. They are proud of what they have achieved but don't feel the need to brag about it.

They haven't gotten where they are by applying some amazing money-making scheme. It's understanding their relationship with money and aligning their values, beliefs, and behaviours that have led them to financial success. They have high self-esteem, feel secure, and are content with life.

So where are you right now? Are there any attributes in one of the other money personalities that you would like to take on?

Money Mastery is what we all aspire to be. Unfortunately, most people either aren't willing to do the work (or don't know how) to get there.

Why Do You Need To Know Your Money Personality?

You aren't stuck in one personality type forever. If you took the Money Personality Quiz (www.moneymentalist.com) again in a year's time, it may well be different because you are in a different stage of life or something has changed how you relate to money. For example, you might be a Spender now–then you fall in love with a Hoarder and want to go on an overseas trip with your new partner. Your motivation to start saving for the trip could move you towards the Hoarder personality.

Once you understand what your money personality is and how you move between personality types depending on life circumstances, you can make a conscious choice to move between the types as you need to.

Just one point here: please don't consciously move into Avoider mode; that is the one personality style we want to spend as little time in as possible.

The other part of knowing your money personality is that it helps you understand what you are *doing* right now.

It is very easy to use our money personality to justify our actions as I did. "I'm a spender, that's just what I do' was my mantra. Once I realized this mantra wasn't helping me and was in fact causing me a great deal of financial pain, I was able to look more objectively at what I was doing and decide to make a change.

It's a bit like looking in the mirror and not liking what you see so deciding to change the way you eat...

If you want a different result, your behaviour is part of the process of change. It's the middle part of my favourite equation:

Beliefs drive *behaviours* drive results.

Your money personality, your emotions, and your money biases all feed into the *behaviours* part of the equation. Understanding how they all fit together and what impacts your behaviour positively or negatively helps you make better choices to get you where you want to go.

Understanding behaviour is really important, but even more important is understanding the *why*–your money beliefs and the money stories you tell yourself from those beliefs.

Knowing what I know now, looking back, I can see very clearly that I was (and still am) an Amasser/Spender money personality. I was a business owner with my own accounting practice and Gaz and I also had an investment in a café. Gaz was also an Amasser, but his secondary personality was Avoider. He was happy for me to look after all of our finances (business and joint personal). He never asked about our situation and I never shared. Neither of us had much Hoarder personality so we didn't take much notice of what was happening. Gaz assumed that as I was the accountant, I had it all under control. Which I didn't. But I was feeling ashamed that I didn't so I just continued juggling to make things work as best I could on my own. Gaz trusted me with our finances and I avoided the hard conversations, like continuing to pay rent on his apartment in Sydney when we really couldn't afford to.

We spent money to make ourselves feel better without thinking about the consequences, hence the puppy!

I also had an underlying belief that I could have anything I wanted, when I wanted, regardless of whether or not I could afford it. This fed into my money behaviours at the time as well. I never said no to anything we wanted to do, from going out to dinner, to a trip back to Sydney for a weekend. We weren't extravagant, but we were definitely living beyond our means.

As I discovered in our hospice conversations, Gaz was also feeling ashamed that he wasn't providing enough income, but he didn't know how to talk about that either, and as his nature was to withdraw, that's what he did.

We both acknowledged that we had put our heads in the sand hoping the problem would magically fix itself. And for a while, that strategy worked as property prices were increasing so we borrowed more from the bank and used that to fund our lives.

The crazy thing was that there was no way I would recommend that as a strategy to any of my accounting clients. Yet, I happily did it in my own life.

As you may have seen from my own story, understanding your *why* is so foundational to your money relationship that we will spend the next chapter exploring your money beliefs.

CHAPTER 2

WHERE DOES YOUR RELATIONSHIP WITH MONEY COME FROM?

Before we go any further, pause for a moment and think about money. What is the first word that pops into your head? That word is the primary meaning money has for you.

Write this word down in your journal as we'll come back to it in Chapter 4.

To me, money means ____.

We are going to unpack where that meaning came from, so you can decide if it still serves you well today or if it needs a bit of a refresh.

Our Money Beliefs

We need to start by understanding what a belief is. Here is a nice simple definition that I think sums up a belief well.

A belief is an assumed truth that we then turn into a reality. It becomes a self-fulfilling prophecy.

Some beliefs are easier to spot than others; they are out in the open for all to see. Some beliefs can be quite polarising, for example, religious and cultural beliefs. You can see these kinds of beliefs playing out quite clearly in the world of politics as well. These beliefs appear on the surface, as we are quite happy to talk (or protest) about them, but they also run very deep in our psyche.

Some of the not-so-obvious beliefs that also run deep are around our body image and how we think we should look, diet, what we think we should eat, and of course, money. These beliefs sit in the subconscious until something happens, or we are challenged in some way, and realise that we have this particular belief. You can then make a decision: do you want to keep it and continue to live with it? If the belief is working for you then the answer is probably yes! Or, do you want to toss it out and replace it with a new one? If the belief causes you stress or anxiety, you probably want to review it.

You also need to bear in mind that your beliefs are personal to you. Just because you have a personal belief about something doesn't mean that everyone else thinks the same way. You and someone else with totally different beliefs can get the same results.

For example, one couple believes that having a stay-at-home parent is best for the family. Another couple believes that both parents working is best for the family. Both families are happy and have great relationships with each other. Neither set of beliefs is right or wrong. It is all about your beliefs and the beliefs of those who are closest to you working together and being in alignment.

Think of something that is both important to you and something you do. An easy area to think about is diet, health, and fitness. Do you eat (or not eat) a certain way because you believe it is better for you? Do you do a particular type of exercise? Sometimes these beliefs support us and are in alignment with reality. Other times an underlying belief can become a self-fulfilling prophecy through our behaviour.

Here's an example. I had asthma as a child and was unable to run without having an asthma attack. From that experience, I have a belief that I will never run a marathon. I have never challenged that belief by attempting a marathon, and even though I no longer have asthma, I will never run. I don't own a pair of running shoes and I've never been tempted to buy any. My belief has become a self-fulfilling prophecy–because I believed that asthma prevented me from running, I've never ran. Maybe I would have been capable to run, but I allowed my belief to become my reality. In the scheme of things, this is not a significant belief; it doesn't bother me at all. On the other hand, I love walking. My grandmother still walks every day at the age of 98, my mother walks every day, and guess what? So do I. I have a belief that walking is good for me, so I happily engage in that activity. This belief has *also* become a self-fulfilling prophecy. At my annual physical checkup, my doctor confirms that I am fit and healthy. This is proof enough for me that this belief is working for me.

Now it's your turn. Think of something you do habitually in any area of life. Maybe it's the way you stack the dishwasher. Why do you stack it the way you do? How did it become a 'thing' you do? There is an underlying belief about why you do it that way.

I'm not sure where I heard this story, but it is so lovely, I am going to share it with you.

A newly married couple (let's call them Sue and John) are having the first extended family Christmas dinner together. Sue is preparing the leg of lamb ready to roast (yes, this is a Kiwi story), and diligently cuts off the end piece of the roast before putting it in the oven. John peers over her shoulder and asks why she did that. 'Well', she replies, a little indignant, 'that's how you prepare a lamb roast'. Not wanting to upset his wife or start an argument, John leaves her to it. But he can't let it go, so he has a quiet chat to his Mum, and she's a bit puzzled as well as she doesn't do it this way.

After a lovely Christmas lunch and emboldened with a couple of glasses of wine, John approaches his mother-in-law and asks about the lamb leg preparation. She laughs and says she has always done it that way, as when she was growing up, her Mum did it that way because the leg of lamb wouldn't fit in her roasting dish. She had to chop the end bone off which has now become a family tradition and ritual.

John decides to say nothing to Sue about this but resolves that next year he will prepare the lamb roast so he can enjoy all of it!

The moral of the story is that sometimes we do things because that's just the way it's always been done. We don't think about it because it works for us, but what if it doesn't? What do we do then? We can choose to continue doing what we've been doing, because even an uncomfortable comfort zone is comfortable, or we can choose to explore *why*.

Now think about whether you have ever done anything to challenge that belief. Practice a few other things that you *do*, then move on to the things that you *think*. These may be harder to identify. You will know that they are deeply held beliefs if you've never done anything to challenge them.

Where Do Our Beliefs Come From?

Our beliefs are not just about money, but also how we use language and form our view of the world, all start with our early childhood memories and the beliefs we formed from those observations. We can still hold onto those beliefs and make our decisions based on our childhood worldview, in my case, as a 4-year-old. As we get older some of our beliefs will drop away and we will add new ones to our repertoire. Some will be modified and others will become more entrenched. This all happens subconsciously; we aren't aware that it's happening unless something comes along that challenges our beliefs

My earliest memories of money revolve around the word 'No'. No, I couldn't have the pink umbrella with the frill, the must-have winter fashion accessory for a 4-year-old. No, I couldn't have a Barbie doll, they were too expensive, so I got the imitation one instead. From my 4-year-old perspective, it was not the same, but to my parents it was.

My parents' goal was to own their home mortgage-free, and to their credit, they achieved that. But it meant that we moved house a lot, and with each move, we traded down so the mortgage kept getting smaller. By the time I was at university they were debt-free and have been ever since. That is well over 40 years now.

What money beliefs did I learn from this?

1. Be careful with your money.
2. You don't need an extravagant lifestyle and the best of everything—you're often paying for the label when the imitation can be just as good.
3. It's all about practicality and functionality.

That belief worked well for me whilst I was living at home. I diligently saved most of my wages from my after-school job, which enabled me to buy my first car. I was a Hoarder personality back then.

Then the inevitable happened; I left home and started working full time.

I remember spending most of my first pay packet on the most beautiful sheepskin rug (Okay, I'm a New Zealander and we are surrounded by sheep!). My parents were horrified. I was so proud of myself and my new possession.

The next week it was something else, and then I was on the slippery slope of buying stuff; I discovered credit cards, and for many years after that everything my parents had instilled in me disappeared out the window. I never did tell them the size of the mortgage I had on my own home!

You see, my belief about money changed. I didn't realise it at the time, but I went from being careful with money to being careless with money. Put another way, I went from being a Hoarder to a Spender!

It was only when I really started challenging my beliefs that I realised there was much more to my parents' careful Hoarder attitude toward money.

They were careful with their money so they could manage with my Dad's income and Mum could be a stay-at-home mum. They didn't waste money on 'stuff', they saved it so I could have a great education and we could have family holidays together.

As a result of having to explore my own behaviours and beliefs about money, I have come full circle. I am very clear about what I value in life and how I choose to use my money. My decisions are thought through more carefully in terms of the big picture and the financial and life goals that are now in place. Yes, I still love nice things, but rather than buy on impulse I choose when I want to hoard and when I want to spend, and I always ask the question: *Is spending this money adding joy and value to my life?* If yes, I buy, if no, I don't. If I'm not sure, I give myself more time to decide.

Now it's your turn. I encourage you to take some quiet time, get out your journal, and think and write about your earliest memories of money in your childhood, I want you to capture your initial thoughts– don't try and deep dive, you can do that later. All you need to write now are short sentences or bullet point answers these questions:

Can you identify a money belief you took from that situation?

Do you think this early money belief changed over the years? Or has it been reinforced?

Included in the bonus workbook you can do the deep work of exploring more about your money memories, the beliefs and stories that you've told yourself about them, and how you feel about them now. You can access the bonus workbook and exclusive readers free gifts by heading to
www.moneymentalist.com/bookbonus

Who Is in Charge of Your Financial Decisions?

This may seem a strange question to ask. The obvious answer is 'Me'! I am in charge, and I make my own financial decisions.

But what if there is more than one of you? Unless you have an identical twin, this also seems an odd question. We all have an inner child and sometimes this is the version of you running not only your financial decisions but your life decisions as well.

Let me explain. When you examine your beliefs, you will still be living some of them from your childhood view of the world. As adults, it's important we listen to our inner child. Our inner child reminds us when it's time to slow down, relax and step back from our adult busy, and often stressful life and have some fun, and do things like go to the beach, walk in nature, and take time out with friends and family. But sometimes our inner child's view of the world holds us back due to fear or anxiety and stops us from doing things in our best interest. What if a childhood belief is impacting your life? What do you do then?

When you find yourself in a financial mess (or any other unhealthy situation in life) it's time to examine those beliefs and ask yourself, 'Who is running my life'? which is exactly what I did.

My four-year-old self who didn't get the Barbie grew into an adult, and somewhere and somehow along the way, I took every no and turned them into *yes*. Yes, I *could* have the beautiful sheepskin rug (purchased with my first week's wages). Yes, I *could* have the new car (rather than fix the stereo in my current one). Yes, I *could* have the diamond earrings (they are really lovely and I do wear them a lot). And yes, I *could* borrow another $10,000 to visit my daughter in Argentina even though I was already $600,000 in debt. The list goes on and on.

My rational adult mind kept giving in to the emotional four-year-old who wanted everything and wanted it NOW! (I like to call this a Freddy Mercury moment). It took a long time and a lot of work on myself and my relationship with money for me to realise what was going on.

But once I had that realisation, it wasn't too difficult to make the changes I needed. Each time I had to make a financial decision, I consciously checked in with myself and asked, 'Who is making this decision? Adult Lynda or Little Lynda'?

Most of the time it needs to be Adult Lynda; *she* needs to be in charge of my financial future, not the emotional four-year-old. But when it comes to fun and play, Little Lynda gets a say as well.

At some point, if you want to become a Money Master, you have to examine your own money beliefs and pay attention to who is making your decisions. It's time to pull out your journal and build on the previous question about your earliest memory of money and the belief you took from that. Answer the following two questions being very honest with yourself in your answers.

1. Who is making the bulk of your financial decisions?

and

2. Are these decisions working for you?

These questions don't just apply to your personal finances; the same beliefs could be impacting your business as well. If you are repeating the same things and not getting the results that you want, or you keep getting stuck and feel frustrated, it may not be the adult you who is in charge.

It is time to take control and let your inner child do what they do best, which is to have fun and put the adult behind the wheel of your financial life.

How Are You Using Money To Communicate?

As we start to understand what money means to us, and what our underlying beliefs about money are, it shouldn't come as a surprise that we use money to communicate as well.

Go and have a look in the mirror–who do you see? Yourself. We are the ones who make money complicated. We are the ones who add emotion and meaning to money and become the authors of our own money stories. And we choose how to write them.

Before you can really knuckle under and start making money simply about math and getting ahead in life, you need to understand how you add emotion and meaning and consequently, how you communicate that.

Let me explain what I mean by giving you a few examples.

What do you think when you go to buy a new car? I heard this from a business owner. 'I can't drive an old car, what would my clients think'?

This statement has very little to do with clients; it's what the business owner wants to communicate with the car they drive. 'I am successful' or 'This car will make others respect me' or maybe even 'I worked hard for this car; I deserve it'. The client, on the other hand, may be thinking, *If they can afford a car like that, I am paying them too much*. The car is the same, but the interpretation is different depending on who you are. These self-statements stem from your personal experiences and point of view.

Money is often seen as either good or bad. We see rich people flaunting their wealth and being obnoxious in the media. That is one perception, but we can also use money to show we care. The list of well-known super-rich business owners who give back and use their money to help others is getting longer. Bill Gates, Richard Branson, and MacKenzie Scott are just a few who spring to mind. But you don't need to be rich and famous to use money to show you care, simply giving some coins to a young musician busking shows appreciation and care.

We can also use money to control and manipulate others. This isn't just in the realm of the super-rich. I come across this quite a lot when working with separated couples. The emotions surrounding a relationship breakup can bring out quite interesting money behaviours, ranging from completely withholding money from the ex-partner to force them into a settlement to showering children with money in hope that they will 'change sides' or to giving the ex-partner everything in the hope they will come back.

Now it's your turn. Think about some of the ways you use money to communicate. Buying your partner a present to say 'I'm sorry' after a fight. Paying for all of your friends meals to celebrate your new job. Even the food you put in your trolley at the supermarket shows your communication style with money.

This is not about judging yourself or others for how they use money to communicate. This is about building your own awareness of how you use it and then asking yourself these three questions (which you will see repeated a number of times as we examine your money story and beliefs). It's time for a bit of journalling.

1. Why am I doing this?
2. What money belief is this coming from?
3. Is this working for me or not?

What's Your First Memory of Earning Money?

I saw a poll on LinkedIn that I found interesting; the poll asked what our first job was. I think we can all remember our first job, maybe it was a paper run before school, working in a shop during the holidays, or your first experience after you graduated from university.

My question is a little different. I want to know what your first memory was of *earning* money. This may not have been a job. You might have received pocket money based on the chores you did at home. I know some parents reward their children with money when they pass an exam or reach some other milestone achievement. You might have been like me, I started my first business at the age of nine knitting jumpers for a tourist shop. You might have a similar story.

I would like you to take this memory and use it as the basis for one of your Money Stories. Writing Money Stories is something we dig into much more deeply in Part Three. If something jumps out at you now, then write about it, if not, don't worry. Something may come to you as you continue to read.

If you do want to write this story now, pull out the journal and find some quiet time and start writing. Get really detailed and take yourself back to that time. What happened? When was it? Who was there with you? Think about it as if you were writing the script for a movie. How did you feel when you got paid? Elated? Disappointed? Then what did you do with that money? Spend it? Save it? Did you continue doing whatever it was to earn more money? Or did you stop or do something different?

As you write and reflect on this story, you will see multiple beliefs come through. Some beliefs will be about money and some may be around work ethic or your value in the marketplace. It's a good idea to capture your thoughts about your beliefs in these areas as well.

If anything has come up for you, look at your list and see which ones you still believe. Are these beliefs working for you? If yes, keep doing them. If no, then what do you want to replace that belief with? What is getting in your way of changing that belief?

Remember, beliefs appear to be real, but in fact, we create them and then live into them. You can always change your mind and write a new story. This is probably a good place to touch on the law of attraction and manifestation. Yes, I do believe that you can attract money to you by utilising positive money beliefs. I have a couple of friends who are very good at doing this. But, there is another side to the law of attraction and that is the law of action! Sitting on the couch wishing for money to appear won't get you there. Sitting on the couch, allowing amazing thoughts to come into your head, and then acting on them *will*.

While we are talking about earning money, it's probably a good time to let you know you also have a **money ceiling**.

What's Your Money Belief Ceiling?

Our money beliefs will determine how much income we think we are capable of earning. That is what I call the Money Belief Ceiling. Once you hit that ceiling, unless you change your money beliefs, you will not progress any further. You will subconsciously push money away that exceeds that ceiling.

So, if we have a money belief ceiling, we also have a money floor. Our money floor is our current income. We can increase our income and raise our floor, but if we don't address our money belief ceiling, we will hit it and go no further.

This can happen very quickly if we come into money unexpectedly. For example, winning the lottery or a business suddenly taking off and exceeding all expectations can cause the same problem. We don't have the money beliefs that allow us to accept that we *can* have that much money, so we will push it away. This may be in the form of a spending spree and buying lots of 'toys' or giving money away or making bad business decisions that result in losing money. There are also non-financial ways we push money away as well. You might find yourself arguing with your partner more than usual.

How do you know what your money belief ceiling is? Think about how much income you earn now, and then multiply that by 20. When you think of that number, what is the first thought that comes into your head?

If it's something like *I could never earn that much money* then you are over your ceiling. Do the exercise again, multiply your current income by 10, then five, once you get a point where you feel comfortable and the thought is, *That's achievable,* then you are within your ceiling of belief.

If you want to raise your money belief ceiling, you need to determine what your money beliefs are: examine them, challenge them, and change them. I worked with a client who had a money belief ceiling that was holding her back from growing her business. As we worked together she identified that she had a money belief that you couldn't be rich *and* good. This is a common belief. She was scared that money would change her in some way, so she was holding herself and her income back. This belief came from childhood and what she had seen and heard her family say when a relative 'came into money'. We challenged the story–was it really valid in her world today? As a child, we may only hear snippets of conversations and yet we build our whole life story from this. Fortunately, my client was able to talk to her mother about this belief and learn that she had misinterpreted the conversation. Once she realised that, it was very easy to rewrite the "I can't be rich and good' story to "I can be a rich, generous, and loving person' because that is who she was and still is. Her business income doubled within months. She valued herself and her skills more in the marketplace and put her consulting rate up, gained better clients, worked less, and enjoyed her business more.

Now it's your turn. Take a few minutes now and work out where your money ceiling is. How far from it are you? Do you have room to grow? Or have you hit it and see yourself pushing money away? Once we hit our money ceiling, we will self-sabotage to bring us back down to our comfort level. This could be an unexpected bill that takes the money back out of your bank account.

It can even impact your relationship. One husband observed that when his wife got a bonus from work, they seemed to argue more. It was as if she was pushing him away until the bonus was all spent.

Looking back, I can see how in my relationship with Gaz we had probably both hit our money ceilings. Not that we would have known about it or understood it. My accounting business had plateaued and his income had gone down, rather than up. Fortunately for us, our business partner in the café hadn't hit her money ceiling and she was continuing to grow the café revenue. The cafe was enabling us to prop up our lifestyle and avoid having to look at our own businesses.

A money ceiling applies in business as well. I had a client in the construction industry on a five-year rollercoaster cycle. The profits would grow in years one to four and then in year five something would happen (one time it was a client who went bust so they didn't get paid) and they would be back at the start of the cycle. The most extreme event of self-sabotage was starting to construct a building in the wrong place!

So much could have been avoided in this client's business, and in my relationship with Gaz, if we'd all known about money ceilings, floors, and the beliefs that determine them. In the next chapter, we'll look at the money stories holding us back.

CHAPTER 3

WHAT MONEY STORIES ARE HOLDING YOU BACK?

We've talked about beliefs and how they impact our relationship with money. These beliefs come from our money stories, and our money stories help form our beliefs. They are intertwined with each other. We have a belief and we tell ourselves a story. Something happens so we tell ourselves a story which either confirms or reframes our beliefs. Once you understand what your money stories are, you will be able to see your beliefs and identify which beliefs and stories are holding you back. You may be stuck in old patterns of behaviour or an old money belief from childhood could be getting in the way.

When life is going well, we generally don't need to challenge our beliefs or stories, as they are obviously working for us. But when life isn't going so well, we get to a breaking point where we need to do something as the issue is causing us too much pain (emotionally) to continue. Typically, the first place we look is at our behaviour.

Here's an example from a client I worked with.

My client had stopped opening her mail; it was just too hard to face the bills, so she put her head in the sand and let them pile up. She was forced to face reality when her credit card stopped working and her power got cut off. Something was definitely not working for her.

I asked her the following three questions that you will also ask yourself when you are examining your own behaviours.

1. What have you *done*? This isn't the story you tell yourself; this is actually, *what have you done?* In the example above, she had stopped opening mail because she was scared of how much money she'd spent.

2. What are you *doing*? Quite often the answer to this question is *nothing*, you simply aren't dealing with the issue, you're just carrying on as if it isn't there, hoping it will all just go away.

3. What are you *going* to do? This gets to the action point or the behaviour change. Opening the mail would be a start, seeking advice from a money mentor (which is why she was sitting in my office), and getting some sound financial advice are all good starting points.

But it doesn't stop there; this is the first part of your money story: addressing the behaviour that got you to where you are now.

It was quite clear that being an ostrich wasn't working. We could address the practical side of opening mail and putting a plan in place to get her finances back on track, but we also had to deal with the underlying belief about how she got into this muddle so she could recognise the signs and not go there again.

As we worked together, we identified some key beliefs and stories that were holding her back. Here is one of them.

As a child her father managed the household money, as her mother (apparently) wasn't capable of looking after it. From this, the belief emerged that as a woman, she couldn't look after money. This was reinforced in her relationships where her partner always looked after the finances, even in her business.

So when she found herself on her own, she lived out of the story that she was hopeless with money. It became a self-fulfilling prophecy.

Once she realized that this story that she was incapable with money was no longer serving her, she was able to turn it around and replace it with a new belief that she was a competent money manager. With some tools and coaching, she *did* become a competent money manager and took control of her own decision-making for her personal and business finances and hasn't looked back. She rewrote her story from being incompetent to being very capable.

This isn't an easy process and is not one for the faint-hearted. Your beliefs and your stories have been around for a long time, so don't expect them to suddenly change overnight just because you learn something new. These stories have formed your habits–you have to continue to reinforce the new beliefs into new stories so the process of change can occur.

Here are some common money stories:

'I don't deserve money.'

'Money grows on trees.'

'People with a lot of money aren't nice people.'

'Rich people are greedy.'

'I'm creative, so I'll never be good with money, or have any!'

There are many more.

Your underlying belief about money impacts all of your decisions. They influence how you perform and whether or not you will achieve your goals. And, as I mentioned earlier, they become self-fulfilling prophecies because we live what we believe. As they are buried in your subconscious you may not even be aware of what they are.

Now it's your turn. Off the top of your head, what common money stories are popping into your mind right now? Write them down so you are ready to explore them further in Part Three.

There are two types of beliefs that feed your money story:

1. *Empowering beliefs* are the ones that say, 'I can do this".

2. *Limiting beliefs* say, 'I'm not good enough'.

Empowering beliefs are the ones that move you forward. You want more of these in your life. These are beliefs that start with:

I will... make a plan and follow it.

I believe... that I make good decisions.

I can... make the money I need or find a way to love my work.

I am... competent and know what I am doing to achieve my goals.

Limiting beliefs are the ones that hold us back, that have us doubting ourselves and our abilities, and also impact our behaviour and our emotional wellbeing. They sound like this:

I will never... make the money I need.

I feel stuck... in repeating dumb behaviour.

No matter what I do... nothing will change.

I can't... see how I can change my life.

My opinion... doesn't matter.

As you begin to change your beliefs, you begin to write a new money story.

Every belief also has a point of reference, known as a locus of control. The term 'locus of control' refers to how much control a person feels they have in their own behaviour. A person can either have an internal locus of control or an external locus of control (Rotter, 1954). To initiate change you must move your locus of control from external to internal.

If you have a high *internal* locus of control, you see yourself as having a great deal of personal control over your behaviour and are therefore more likely to take responsibility for your own actions and results. You are also prepared to make tough decisions when you need to. For example, I have emergency and savings money for a rainy day because I saved for them. Or, I have no savings because I choose to spend all my earnings on doing things and buying stuff.

If you have high *external* locus of control, you look outside of your own actions and tend to see your behaviour as being a result of external influences or luck– for example, I wouldn't have saved if my parents hadn't made me... You'll see failures as being due to bad weather or the economy or some other factor out there. It's about not taking responsibility for your own actions. I often hear this one. It isn't me who spends the money, it's my wife/husband!

As you can see from my client's story above, not only did she change her beliefs and her story about money, but she also shifted her locus of control as well.

Now it's your turn. If something isn't working for you (financially or non-financially), pay attention to what you are thinking. Write notes in your journal about these questions.

Are you feeling empowered or limited?

Can you do something about it or is it out of your control?

If you realise your mindset is tending toward the negative, start to challenge your belief around your problem. Look for proof that debunks the belief. This is something you can work on every time something's not feeling right or you feel frustrated about not being able to get where you want to go in life. Affirmations, vision boards, and meditation, to name a few, are great practices to help you challenge and change your beliefs.

A final point to remember: **Change is a process, not an event.** Don't expect instant success. Breakthroughs rarely happen over breakfast one morning. Instead, it's often a process so gradual that you may not even be aware that your beliefs are steadily but surely taking on a new positivity.

The way to know that you are making progress is to have a clearly defined starting point to use as a reference when you check in on yourself. Setting an appointment to check in with your finances, like how much debt you have versus previously or reflecting on your money behaviour then versus now, is a tangible way to see growth. For example, if you were an impulse spender, check in with yourself three months later–do you spend impulsively as often as before? Why or why not? **This is a great opportunity to celebrate wins and challenge stubborn beliefs that still need attention.**

If you are feeling stuck and just don't seem to be able to move forward, think of it this way: there are two driving forces in human nature. One is the desire to seek pleasure and the other is the desire to avoid pain. What pain are you avoiding? What keeps you firmly in your comfort zone (even though it may not be comfortable)? This is a great journalling exercise, not just about money, but any area of your life that is troubling you.

You may need to have a look at your environment–what and who is surrounding you? Both may be influencing your behaviour. Think of a TV shows like The Biggest Loser. In the controlled environment of the show the contestants do very well at losing weight through diet and exercise. Yet when they go back to their old environments after the show, many unfortunately put the weight back on.

I watched a documentary about an Australian man who had a long hospital stay in a very controlled environment to lose weight. After he made some good progress he returned home. His parents didn't understand nor support him in his continuing effort to lose weight. He knew that if he stayed, all of his effort to get healthy would be lost. He decided he had no other option but to cut off contact with his parents. This was the hardest decision to make, but he did it for the sake of his health.

You may not have to do something as drastic as this, but maybe getting rid of a few credit cards and saying no to friends who want to go out all the time is a decision you need to make for your financial health.

We can also use the excuse of not knowing how to do something to justify our behaviour. If you don't know how to manage money, you can easily solve that by learning how. We can all learn new skills if we want to, so if you don't know how to do something, go and find someone to teach you. Feeling more capable is a very good way to start changing your beliefs and your stories.

Stop telling yourself stories that don't support your goals and vision for the future. Take action.

It's time for a bit of soul-searching; be totally honest with yourself and have a look at where you are at this point in your life.

Are you where you want to be in your finances? Your health and well-being? If you are feeling a 'no' bubbling up, then it is time to delve into your behaviours, your beliefs, and your stories and see what changes need to be made. Use the deep-dive exercises in Part Three to help you do this.

CHAPTER 4

MONEY IS EMOTIONAL

Before we even start talking about how you behave with your money, you need to understand that money is emotional. We forget that money is simply a tool that enables us to acquire what we want. Instead, we use money to meet our emotional needs, for example, spending when we are sad to feel better. Or buying an expensive suit thinking it will give us more confidence in a job interview, investing in a get rich quick scheme believing it will work out okay for us, or that having lots of money will make us happy.

We also give money meaning. When it comes to money, one plus one can equal anything we want it to because of the meaning and emotion we attach to it.

During the time when my business was struggling and we were battling to keep the café, my emotions were all over the place. Logic had well and truly left the building. I was continuing to spend in both the business and our life as if everything was okay. My head was totally buried in the sand. When I did engage my accountant brain and looked at the reality of our situation and what would happen if we lost the café, it was just too scary. So, I bought another case of wine to add to our cellar and carried on. I wasn't ready to face reality, and I wasn't ready to acknowledge that as an accountant, I was failing badly in my own business and life... that came much later.

In Chapter 2 I asked you to write down the first word that popped into your head when you thought about money. What was your word? When you came up with that word, you might not have thought of it as emotional or have connected how the word impacts the way you use money. It's only as you begin to think about your word more, and how you use it, that you will begin to see the pattern of emotion and meaning showing up.

Below are some of the answers I've heard when I asked my clients 'What does money mean to me?' The most common answers are first, followed by a couple of others just to get you thinking. These answers tend to signal to us the meaning we have attached to money.

Love

'I work so hard, I'm never home, so I make up for it by buying the children lots of gifts.' This is a common scenario for working parents who use money to show love, or as a substitute for love, towards their children so they feel less guilty themselves.

Power

'It's my business so it's my money, and I make all the decisions.' Money, position, and power are a dynamic combination, and have been used to control others so that (in theory) they do what you want them to do.

Security

'I want to feel secure when I retire, know that I can go to the doctor when I need to, spoil the grandchildren a little, and do the things I want to do.' This client wants financial security which can be measured by how much they have in their retirement fund and in the bank. Knowing what that number is for you will give you the financial security you are seeking.

Freedom

'Money will make me free. I won't have to work, I can pay off all my debt, travel, and enjoy life.' Certainly, having money over and above our day-to-day needs does give us a sense of freedom as our range of choices and what we can do increases. But it's what we do with that freedom that matters.

Independence

'When I get a job, I can leave home and become independent and do my own thing.' It's an emotional day for parents when our children leave the nest and go out into the big wide world. Some of them fly straight away, others have a bumpy ride and need a bit more support. Money may increase the possibility for independence but it's not a guarantor of it.

Dependent

'I am totally dependent on my partner (family) for money, so I can never take a risk or do what I want.' This is a sad and difficult place to be. Feeling unable to express yourself because of the fear of being cut off financially can be stifling. Feeling trapped can make it difficult to take positive action steps to become free of the financial bond.

Worthy

'Making money makes me feel good. I have proved my family wrong; I am not stupid, and now they are proud of me.' Some of us use money to build our self-esteem and prove to others that we are worthy. But what about you, are *you* proud of yourself and your achievements, or will you keep making more money to please everyone else? You can't equate self-worth with your net financial worth, but frequently the two get confused.

Fear

'I'm scared of making a wrong decision and losing money, of not having enough in my bank account to pay my bills". This fear can spill into other areas of life, not only creating financial anxiety, but general anxiety as well. It can stop you enjoying life to its fullest.

Shame

'I know I should have more savings/equity in my house/balance in my retirement fund to show for all the income I have earned over the years. I just don't know where it has all gone". We feel shame when we don't live up to an internal ideal. Those ideals come from family, friends, and what we see in the media about what we 'should' have or be. We tend to keep shame to ourselves.

For all of these meanings, and any others that you come up with, I would like you to contrast this with emotional security. This is the feeling that having money will make you feel good, satisfied with your life, or fulfill some other emotional need. The problem with this is that when money is scarce, we lose our sense of emotional stability.

Money shouldn't have this power.

It *can't* be the source of your emotional needs.

Money can't turn you into whom you want to be, you are still the same person on the inside.

I think this quote from David Krueger (*The Secret Language of Money*) and my mentor is very powerful and worth remembering. 'Money can make any statement, carry any message, and represent any notion. Money is like an object in a dream. It can mean anything we ask it to mean.'

Now it's your turn. You have your word—expand that into a couple of sentences as in the examples above. If you can come up with some examples of how that has impacted a financial decision you have made, write that down as well.

So what was my word? Back in the days when Gaz and I were together, money meant self-worth and self-esteem to me. It was all about proving myself worthy to myself and others. I had the nice car and the jewelry. I had the latest software in my business (not that it ever got used), I went to all the conferences, and organized activities with my team.

Gaz and I never spoke about what money meant to us, as we just didn't talk about money at all. Looking back, I think Gaz and I lived from a belief that money meant freedom. He had done the long hours in the corporate world and been very successful. I think his word was about power and success. But after two heart attacks in his 30s and bypass surgery in his 40s, his whole view of the world changed. I noticed after his bypass surgery that he lost the drive to push himself to succeed in business. He slowed down in all areas of life and wanted to spend more time making music, researching, and taking on projects he knew he needed in order to have some income. And he trusted me to ensure that between us we had enough.

The Oxford Dictionary defines money as a noun: 'A current medium of exchange in the form of coins and banknotes'.

Interesting definition. As you can see from the sample answers to 'What does money mean to me?' above, none of the answers referred to coins, notes, or even credit cards. Money means so much more to us than that, and that meaning is reflected in our beliefs, our behaviours, and our results.

Take some time and think again about what money means to you. Then ask yourself *why* it means that to you.

This underlying meaning impacts your financial decisions. If money means security to you, then you will make different choices than someone whose primary meaning is power, for example. What money means to you is not set in concrete and it can, and probably will, change over your lifespan.

The main thing to recognise right now is whether your money meaning fits with where you are now in your life. Are you living out of a belief that really doesn't have meaning anymore? This could be why you feel stressed or anxious about money—you are out of alignment between what money means to you, your beliefs about money, and your behaviour with money.

Spending Money and Your Emotions

One of the main drivers to spending money is an emotional trigger. It can be anger, sadness, revenge, happiness, or any other myriad of emotions that have us swiping our credit cards.

Here are a few emotional states that impact our spending behaviour.

Sadness: Feeling sad increases the amount of money we are willing to spend. Sadness can also reduce our patience. It isn't called retail therapy for nothing. Buying stuff can give us a short-term lift (until the credit card bill arrives), but more stuff isn't really what you need when you have the blues. Try exercise or catching up with a friend instead.

Anger: Feelings of anger can either make you take bigger risks or dig your toes in, particularly if challenged. Be wary of making decisions in this emotional state, especially investment decisions or you may find yourself gambling away your retirement fund on speculative stocks that you wouldn't ordinarily invest in.Take a step back and give yourself more time, say 24 hours, before you make major decisions to allow the anger to dissipate.

Scared: Feeling scared has the exact opposite effect of anger. You are more likely to exaggerate the amount of risk, second-guess yourself, and abandon a course of action if it starts to go slightly off track. It can have a positive side–fear of leaving our loved ones behind without a penny can encourage you to buy life insurance. If you feel you are unsure of your next step, or can't quite make a decision, it's time to talk to a trusted adviser. This may be a professional (like me), or a close friend or family member who has the knowledge to help you.

Guilt: We feel guilt when we violate our internal standards. So if you work long hours and don't spend enough time with family, and that is a high value for you, you will feel guilty and may make up for the guilt by buying gifts. It doesn't have to be on material things, it may be on experiences like a night out at a show or a trip. Guilt can also encourage altruism. What can you do to resolve the guilt in a way that doesn't include spending money? Are you able to negotiate some work from home days versus being in the office? Do you need to ask for a payrise? Or even find a new job?

The first thing you need to check in on is your emotional state. How do you feel? If your emotions are heightened, you will likely spend more money than you normally would. Every purchase is an emotional decision. Without a balance of emotional awareness and rationale, our money meaning can kick in, causing our emotions to override our logical self. Then we find we've bought a boat we don't need or even really want. Ever had shopper's remorse?

A client told me this story after we had had a session on money and emotions. He had recently separated from his spouse and his emotions were all over the place. He had been very diligent at checking in with his emotions before spending. He felt proud of his achievements to date. Then one particularly trying day, challenges with his ex-wife left him angry while still in the charge of his two-year-old daughter. He took his daughter to the local department store. He grabbed a trolley and off he and his daughter went, racing round the store, literally grabbing anything they wanted and throwing it into the trolley, muttering expletives under his breath the whole time. After about 15 minutes of this, he calmed down, took a few deep breaths, looked at his daughter, and then calmly walked around the shop putting most of the items back. He recognised that his emotional state of anger was not serving him well, nor was he presenting a good role model for his daughter. He moved into a state of gratitude and they both felt much happier with the few items they did end up purchasing.

Here's another example. If money means status to you and you go to buy a new car, your emotions might anticipate the satisfaction and pleasure you'll feel when you look cool in your new car to the envy of your friends. You're not buying a car, you're buying the status the car gives you according to your money meaning.

Your logical brain, on the other hand, will be saying, 'But the older car we already have will still get us from point A to B just as well.' Who will win, emotions or logic?

On top of that, we have our money personality joining the conversation as well. The Spender personality is probably going to go for the cool look of the new car, whilst the Hoarder will do a bit more thinking about the decision and weigh up the pros and cons, of which the pros will need to be significantly greater. The Amasser could go either way, and the Avoider will probably find making the decision just too hard and will either do nothing or let someone else make the decision for them.

And you thought you were just popping out to buy a car! This process doesn't happen on just big-ticket items, it goes on all the time. Smaller purchases don't usually have as lengthy a debate and can be more automatic and driven by our personality. We don't tend to be in the supermarket consciously analyzing everything we put in the trolley based on what money means to us. But *subsconciously* I am analysing as I look for quality, healthy options, and value for money. All of this links to my values and the significance of money as a source of independence and freedom to me now.

Becoming a hermit might seem like a good option right now, as there doesn't seem to be an emotion that doesn't get us into strife when we want to spend. I have saved the best for last. This is an emotion that we want to be in when spending, and that emotion is gratitude.

Gratitude: Feeling grateful reduces our impatience, making it more likely to practice delayed gratification. We are generally happier when we feel gratitude, enjoying the experience more and taking the time to think, which lets our rational brain kick in before we buy.

So next time you are in a negative emotional state and feel the urge to splurge, stop outside the store you are about to enter or pause on the site of your favorite online shopping and take a few minutes to write down at least five things you are grateful for. You may well find the urge to spend passes. If it doesn't, you will be much happier with what you do buy.

How Do You Know If You Are An Emotional Spender?

First of all, acknowledge, 'Yes! I am an emotional spender!' Some of those emotions will help you make really good decisions and other emotions won't as much.

Recognize the triggers that send you into the emotional state that takes you into the not-so-good spending space.

I'm sure we've all been guilty at one time or another of purchasing something, getting it home, looking at it a day or so later, and asking ourselves, 'Why on earth did I buy that?'

This isn't just a woman thing. Men spend emotionally as well; we may just spend a little differently when emotions get in the way.

How can you tell if your emotions are leading you to not-so-good spending decisions?

What do you do when you feel stressed? Think about the last time you felt under a lot of pressure, did you:

a) Go for a run or walk to clear your head?

b) Reach into the fridge for a glass of wine?

c) Pick up a chocolate bar on the way home and eat it while driving?

d) Head to the closest shopping centre and come home laden with goodies?

e) Head to your local bar and buy a round of drinks for everyone?

Another tell-tale sign of an emotional spender is that you spend regardless of whether you can afford to or not. There may be other bills to pay, but in the heat of the moment, you don't care that the rent is due tomorrow or that the power bill is due next week. You just have to have whatever has caught your fancy.

An emotional spender has mastered the art of storytelling. You can justify your spending till the cows come home. By the time you've finished, you've written a novel about why it was perfectly okay for you to splurge.

For those few minutes when you are trying on the new shoes, your emotions suddenly lift and you feel great. You know everyone is going to admire your new purchase. That high usually lasts until you walk out the door of the shop. Then a little while later (anywhere from minutes to days) buyer's remorse sets in.

Emotional spenders can, from time to time, find themselves in sticky financial situations and have to 'rob Peter to pay Paul' by shuffling money around between credit cards and bank accounts to get ends to meet, or borrow money from friends and family to tide them over. This causes more stress, so guess what? You go spending again and the viscous cycle continues.

I know this cycle because it's one I lived until I had a very public meltdown in a restaurant while having dinner with a client about a year or so after Gaz and I separated! It had all got too much for me and the dam burst, the tears flowed, my client calmly and quietly took me out of the restaurant, and we sat on a park bench that looked out at the sea. My client kindly asked me what was wrong. That was the first time someone had asked me that. I had been so good at putting a brave face on my life and my financial situation, it had to come out at some point.

If you can see yourself in these behaviours, here are a few things you can do to start to bring your emotional spending under control:

1. Recognise which emotion triggers your spending. Next time that emotion hits, make a conscious choice to do something different.

2. Step back and give yourself some time to come back to equilibrium. If you find yourself about to pull out the credit card, stop, count to 10 (higher if you need to), and give your rational brain time to kick in. Then you can really decide if you want to spend the money.

3. Get some support or help from a friend; that's what they are there for. Pick up the phone and, as my daughter says to me, 'have a rant'. It's always best to make sure the timing is okay with them first. Once you have the emotion off your chest, the impulse to spend will have dissipated.

4. Minimise temptation as much as you can. If online shopping is your thing, unsubscribe from emails that will tempt you to spend. Don't save your credit card number on your computer, that way, every time you want to spend, you have to get the card out and enter the number. I have had clients who have put their credit card in a container in the freezer. They have to wait for it to defrost before they can use it. The impulse is well and truly gone by the time the card has thawed!

Can you see any patterns or habits that you can easily change that will make a difference to your emotional spending? This exercise was very enlightening for one of my clients. Her mum was in a Dementia care home and while some visits were really good, others weren't so, and my client felt upset as she drove home. We noticed that on the 'upset' visit days, she would stop at a particular homewares shop that was on her route home and buy something she didn't really need or want. On the 'good' visit days, she didn't do this. So, on top of feeling upset about the visit, she added buyer's remorse and would spend the rest of the day an emotional mess. We talked about other ways to deal with feeling upset and how she could nurture herself when she got home, and we changed the route she drove to visit Mum. Once we did this, the spending (and buyer's remorse) stopped.

What Are Your Values?

The final piece of understanding your relationship with money is about knowing and honouring your values.

Wealth means different things to different people. We are bombarded by images and stories of what wealth should be. We are told that we should have the latest model car, the biggest TV, and travel the world in style. Maybe that isn't you, but you feel pressured to live that way because that's what you think wealth is.

Your wealth comes from your values. Knowing your values and living your values means you will become wealthy, whatever that means to you. Saying no becomes easy when you know your own definition of wealth and are actively creating it.

Values are ideas that we feel are important to how we live our lives. Our values are interwoven with our beliefs.

It is important to understand your values as they should determine your priorities. If you don't know what your values are, you may not understand why you're stressed. For example, if family is one of your core values but you work away from home a lot, you are going to feel stressed because your behaviour isn't aligned with your values.

When I work with clients one-to-one, we determine their values, and then we examine their spending behaviours to see how much in alignment they are with their values.

I did this exercise with a client and about 70% of her spending was not in alignment with her values. One of her core values was health and wellbeing, yet she was spending more on takeaway food than she was on her health. Another core value for her was family; she was spending about 15% of her income on her family in various different ways. We talked about how she felt about that–yes it aligned with her values on the surface, but when we looked at some of what she'd spent she felt she could make better use of that money. So instead of buying her grandson toys every time she visited, she opened up a bank account for him and popped the money there so it could accumulate. This would create the possibility of an adventure together or a long-term savings plan set up by his parents. My client felt so empowered by the decisions she was making and knew being more true to herself and her family would align her spending more with her values.

Now its your turn. Pull out your journal and off the top of your head, what do you think your top five values are? If you don't know, then you need to find out. You can find some online tools and the values questionnaire to help you identify your values in the bonus workbook here www.moneymentalist.com/bookbonus

How values help you in other areas of life

Values exist whether you recognize them or not. Life can be much easier when you acknowledge your values–and when you make plans and decisions that honour them.

When you know your own values, you can use them to make decisions about how to live your life, and you can answer questions like these:

- What job should I pursue?
- Should I accept this promotion?
- Should I start my own business?
- Should I compromise or be firm with my position?
- Should I follow tradition or travel down a new path?

Take the time to understand the real priorities in your life, and you'll be able to determine the best direction for you and your life goals!

It's only since I had to examine my own relationship with money that I have given more than lip service to my values. I would update them every so often, then tuck them away in the drawer and forget about them. I had no idea the importance of them in how I chose to life my life, spend my money, and relate to those closest to me. I was so far out of alignment with my values that it's no wonder my life imploded the way it did.

Now my values are front and centre in my life, I am clear on what they are, and I do my best to ensure that I am living true to those values in my business, my personal life, and my bank account.

When you align your values, beliefs, and behaviour there is no holding you back from achieving your financial goals.

LET'S PULL IT ALL TOGETHER
PART ONE - WRAP UP

Maybe you picked up this book out of curiosity, the title intrigued you, or you are already on your money journey and wanted to learn more. Whatever the reason I am glad you did.

Before moving on to Part Two, let's reflect on what you've learned so far.

Don't forget you can access the bonus workbook and exclusive readers free gifts by heading to www.moneymentalist.com/bookbonus.

The theme of Part One is reflection. You don't know what you don't know, so some of the concepts might have been new to you and maybe even a bit scary to think about, let alone act on. When I am coaching clients, the initial exercises that I do with them are the 'off the top of the head' first thoughts. These are designed to get your thought process going, which I then build on as we work together. I'm following the same approach here with you. As you read, you are capturing your 'off the top of the head' thoughts and will build on those when you do the more detailed exercises in Part Three and in your bonus workbook

We started in Chapter 1 identifying where your relationship with money is right now. You need to find that starting point. If you don't know where you are, how can you make effective choices about where you want to go? What's the first thing a travel agent or Google Maps asks you? Where are you now? Where is the starting point so you can reach your chosen destination? It's the same with your money. If you haven't done the exercises, here's your chance to do them now before moving on. If you already completed the exercise, check in with yourself and see if anything new pops up.

If I was dating money, what would it say about me? Thinking about everything you have learned so far. Here's a slightly different slant on that question: If I was dating money, what do I *want* it to say about me? This is where you get to rewrite your dating story to what you want it to be, not what is currently is.

Your Money Personality – You are welcome to take the quiz again. You may find that you are already seeing something different than the first time around. Here's the quiz: www.moneymentalist.com.

Once you've established where you are now, it's time to look backwards and see how you got to this point in your life. We did this in Chapter 2. This is not an opportunity to beat yourself up, all you are doing is looking back and observing your patterns of behaviour. What *really* happened (not the story you took from that event)?

For me money means _________________. What is the first word that pops into your head? Has your word changed?

What do you do habitually that has become a thing? And why do you do it? This will help you understand where your beliefs come from and how they are formed.

What are your earliest memories of money from your childhood? Can you identify any beliefs from this story?

Who is making your financial decisions? Adult you or child you?

How do you use money to communicate? Can you see any patterns forming?

Have you found your money ceiling? What is the gap between where you are now and where your ceiling is? If you are very close or right on your money ceiling, then lifting your ceiling is what you want to work on. Whatever you call it, manifestation or the law of attraction, it's your belief in yourself and your ability to generate more that will lift that ceiling.

As you start to think more about your beliefs, you will realise some of them no longer serve you. In Chapter 3 we started to identify what those stories are and how empowered (or not) you are feeling to change them.

How long is your list of common money stories? See if you can add a couple more that may have come up as you have been reading.

Have you come up with a situation that is making you feel uncomfortable? It doesn't have to be financial, it could be diet, exercise, or work related. Don't go too deep. This exercise is to help you understand more about the locus of control and how empowered you feel about the situation.

In Chapter 4 we explored more about the emotional connection we all have with money.

Expand your money meaning word into a couple of sentences and examples of how that has impacted your decision making.

It's always good to observe what is going on around you. Once you start to become aware of your own emotional relationship with money you will start to see it showing up in those around you. So, what have you noticed as you've been going about your daily life? What emotions have you felt? What have you seen in your friends and family? Are there emotional connections to money that you may not have noticed before?

Have you got what you think your top five values are written down? Do you think you are living to those values? Is there room for improvement?

Once you have completed all of the exercises, you will have a much clearer understanding about you and your money. You'll be ready to move from the dating phase to a long-term relationship.

This is a really exciting time for you; you are well on your journey to financial success.

So what happens next?

We fall in love, and a whole new journey begins!

YOUR MONEY MINDSET AND RELATIONSHIPS

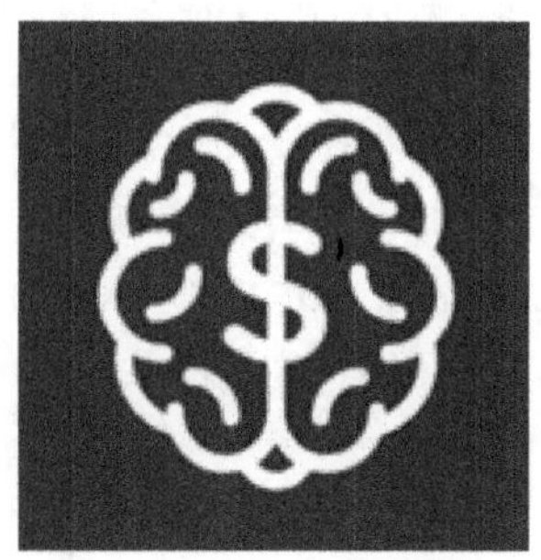

When Gaz and I met, we were both in relationships with other people. He was a newly referred accounting client of mine, and while we had a connection, we focused on business. Not to mention that he was in Australia and I was in New Zealand. Sometime later, both of our relationships had ended and he was visiting New Zealand for a few days. The stars were aligned and we spent nearly every moment of it together.

We both had some trepidation about starting a new relationship, not because of each other but because of our past experiences. I'd already been married three times and each of those had left me more cautious, a bit distrustful, and a little edgy with a new possible partner. So while we were absolutely smitten, we were also aware of our past injuries and our desire to do our next relationship mindfully. He also came from relationships that left him hurt, so we chose to be open pretty quickly about where we hoped the relationship would go.

We had to work through our plans after the long-distance relationship–who would move where? I also had a daughter that locked me into New Zealand, not to mention I had her heart to consider as I navigated this new relationship of mine. We talked through all of these things, and the relationship sailed along beautifully. We even endured Gaz's heart attack and quintuple bypass surgery, bringing us even closer together and showing us what we could withstand as a couple.

We thought we had it all figured out.

But as I shared in Part One, the weight of our individual financial decisions and our conjoint financial decisions, paired with our money mindsets, money personalities, and money beliefs, brought us to the end of our relationship.

We had never been taught how to talk about money. Shoot, even my parents didn't know the amount of debt I was in, how much my business was struggling, nor how my marriage was failing. I kept it all to myself to spare everyone the burden of my hardships, but a little also because I didn't want to admit how much I needed help.

Falling in love with Gaz was easy. Learning how to merge our financial experiences was not. It wasn't enough to talk about how much money we had or who would pay what from where... we needed to dive deep into our expectations, our childhood histories with money, our strengths and weaknesses, and have the hard conversations that can save a marriage.

We didn't. Not until the last weeks of his life. I'll be forever grateful that we'd had enough distance to be raw with each other in those final moments–to see the love that still existed and have the conversations we should've had more than a decade before.

In Part One, we addressed your personal journey with money. In Part Two, we are talking about bringing your unique experience with money into a relationship with someone else's unique experience with money. While my focus is on life partnerships, I also touch on business partnerships. Anytime we bring ourselves into a committed relationship with someone else, business or romantic, we need to be aware of our money mindsets.

That's what we're going to talk about here. I promised Gaz that I would make sure there were as few casualties like ours as possible.

In one of the conversations we had in hospice, as we sat beside each other on the bed, Gaz said something about feeling like his life had been a waste, meaningless, and that he'd achieved nothing. How my heart ached. I told him he was wrong.

'Gaz', I said. 'I thought about what you said, and I disagree. Not only has your life meant something beautiful to so many people (many of whom had regularly visited him in those final weeks), but *Money Mentalist* is your legacy. Everything we have gone through and what we learnt is what I'm taking with me to every client I work with. This will exist because of you. Our story will save so many people what we experienced.

He looked at me, put his head on my shoulder, and said, 'That's pretty huge, isn't it? Thank you'.

Yeah, Gaz, it is.

CHAPTER 5

THEN WE FALL IN LOVE

The first part of the book has been all about you—understanding your relationship with money. We've spent time getting you thinking about your money stories and where they come from, how you behave with money, and what is holding you back. If you worked through the initial exercises in Part One you are going to have a pretty healthy relationship with money. That relationship will improve even more when you do the deep dive exercises in Part Three.

You will have many relationships in your life: parent-child, life partner, business, colleagues, and on and on.

But you will also have a relationship with money.

Your relationship with money is the longest one you will ever have. It's going to outlast every other relationship, so make it strong, make it powerful, and be confident about the choices you are making. You are out of the dating phase with money and are now in a long-term relationship. You know each other pretty well and you are in a good place.

Now think about actual human relationships. You're going along in life, making the most of your singleness, when suddenly, across a crowded room (or dating app), you notice someone. Your eyes meet and, before you know it, you are madly in love!

Maybe you're already in a relationship or maybe you're single waiting for that special someone to come along. But odds are, you're going to get stars in your eyes and meet that special someone.

What happens next? Not only do we bring our own relationship with money into our romantic relationship, but the person we've fallen in love with brings theirs as well! There are now four of you in this relationship. And, as opposites do often attract, the love of your life may be your polar opposite Money Personality.

This is when the fun really starts. Why? Because we have our own stories, we have our money relationship, and we are now merging our money stories and our money relationship, along with everything else (like which order does the cutlery go in the drawer?) together with another person's. Yet we often only think of all the other little decisions that are part of falling in love and building a relationship, like who gets which side of the wardrobe.

I think it's pretty safe to assume that you and your partner didn't wake up one morning, and over coffee and breakfast say, 'Honey, I think we need to talk about our relationship with money and how to merge them'. We just don't. Assumptions about money, power, and gender often remain silent and in the background until something happens and you are forced to address them. For example, if the main breadwinner loses their job and the partners' roles are reversed, one or both of your money stories may become loud fast.

We tend to fall into the patterns of behaviour that we've observed in our history. For example, one young couple I worked with had already achieved a lot in the short time they'd been together. They had a home and good careers but were still unsatisfied. As we talked about this, they realized they were comparing themselves to both sets of parents, who after over 40 years of marriage had accumulated significant assets and were semi-retired. I challenged them to stop living their parents' marriages, focus on their own, and start talking about what they wanted for themselves. They had never done this or even thought about talking about it together. When they did, it turned out it wasn't about accumulating assets, they wanted freedom and travel.

Intentionally bringing your personal money stories into your relationship is important, yet it's one of the hardest things to talk about when you come into a relationship.

We can sort through all of the other stuff, like who cooks on Tuesday. But it's our relationships with money and our ability to bring these together in a positive way that's hard. It was just over 100 years ago that Sigmund Freud said that people find it easier to talk about sex than they do about money. I don't think that that has changed much, even between our nearest and dearest.

Why is that? Again, a lot of it comes from our history. If our parents didn't talk about money, *we* don't necessarily talk about money. We don't know how to talk about it. We're not taught how to have those important conversations during our education. We're not even taught particularly well how to manage our money. We end up learning a lot of money stuff on the fly, and oftentimes through our mistakes. And so has the person you've fallen in love with.

How on earth do you make your money relationship work together as a couple? It doesn't matter whether you've been in a relationship for one year, 10 years, 20 years, or even longer. I meet couples who still struggle with the answer to this question across all time spans. In some ways, for those of you who are in newer, younger relationships, it's easier to address than for those of you who've been in relationships for 10, 15, or 20 years.

Even after seven years together, Gaz and I hadn't learned to discuss money. The result was that Gaz ended up depressed because of feeling worthless due to not being the breadwinner. I had no idea. He was trying to protect me from his financial stress, and I was trying to protect him from mine. Looking back, I now see how this was the opposite of what we needed to do.

In a romantic relationship, two people are closely connected and attuned. Even without words, the other can usually 'read' your mood. We both could see that the other was struggling, but we'd never been taught how to address finances. We attended couple's counselling, and even there we didn't discuss money. Our money stories remained silent. I wish we'd known what I'm teaching you now. No matter what stage of life or relationship you're in, now is the time to start. And I'm going to show you how.

The next part of the book is going to deal with you as a couple, working through your joint money stories and your money behaviour so that you are aligned as a couple and heading in the same direction.

Before we go down that path, let's look at a few areas where men and women are different when it comes to money.

When It Comes to Money – Men And Women Are Different!

Men and women are different; this is no surprise. Ever since John Gray wrote *Men Are from Mars and Women Are from Venus* and Allan Pease wrote about body language, we probably haven't given it much thought.

So, it makes sense that when it comes to money, we are different as well.

Think back historically. There has been a lot of gender bias when it comes to women and money. In the nineteenth century in England, for example, when a woman married, any property she had was legally absorbed by her husband. If she wanted to leave, she had no rights to marital property. The only way she could reclaim property was widowhood! Women (being the weaker and 'fairer' sex) were deemed not competent to handle money, whereas a man was, regardless of his ability. In some countries, there is even now still inequality between men and women and how much they are paid for the same work.

These stereotypes and gender biases have led to a few other differences. Bear in mind that these are generalisations, so not every man or woman is going to fit nicely into these areas. (The following list was compiled by my mentor David Krueger.)

- Men tend to view money as representing power and identity, and women as security and autonomy.

- Men invest to grow the principal, and women to protect it.

- Women investors are less aggressive, trade less, and earn higher returns than men.

- Women worry about losing money more than doing nothing with it. Men don't like inaction, so they are prone to move it around more.

- Women tend to take it personally if they lose investment money. Men tend to blame outwardly–the market, the broker, etc.

- Men orientate towards results. Women put a higher priority on relationship-building, particularly when looking for financial advice.

- Men view effective money management in terms of long-term strategies, e.g. retirement. Women look at short-range goals, e.g finding bargains, eliminating debt, etc.

- If a man earns more than his wife, he tends to think he should have the prime decision-making authority. If reversed, the wife thinks they should have shared democratic decision-making.

Does any of this sound familiar to you?

Where do these differences come from?

A lot of these gender differences are thought to be socio-cultural. In other words, the differences stem from the male characteristics of being the hunter and the female characteristics of being the gatherer and nurturer. Sounds reasonable, but are any of these differences hardwired into our brains?

In 2007 Leonard Sax (a psychologist and family doctor) released his research in the book *Why Gender Matters* (updated in 2017) which included compiling the research of others. Bear in mind that as with any research, there are always differing opinions and Leonard Sax has his fair share of other researchers disagreeing with his findings. This is a snippet of his findings:

A study of newborn babies who had a woman standing on one side of the cot and a revolving mobile on the other found that every newborn boy looked at the mobile, and every girl looked at the woman. This seems to imply a distinct hardwiring between the genders. The conclusion is that men and women are hardwired differently in multiple ways, and these differences start from the womb.

Our eyes are wired differently. Girls look at colour and texture (M cells connected to rods), whilst boys focus on movement (P cells connected to cones).

We hear differently. A girl's hearing is seven times more sensitive than a boy's. By the time we reach adulthood, a woman's hearing is about 24 times more sensitive than a man's. So when a man says, 'I can't hear you', he may well be right!

It does appear from this research that our brains are hardwired differently. Add on top of that stereotypes and socio-cultural differences and it's no wonder we have so much trouble working through the money minefield in our relationships.

Men and Women Spend Differently As Well

How do these differences impact our spending behaviour?

There are a few myths and blind spots that need to be addressed first.

Let's start with the girls. Here are a few lies women might believe:

- Money is too complicated for me to understand.

- Learning about money is boring.

- I don't have enough money or time to do anything about investing.

- If I take a risk, I could lose everything.

- I have to take care of everyone else first.

- We aren't good with money, so I'd better find a man who'll take care of it for me.

- 'Bag Lady Fears'–I might end up out on the street with nothing.

Guys, you don't come off scot-free! You have a few blind spots of your own:

- Managing money is easy.

- If I make more money, I get to make the decisions.

- I don't have to ask my wife/partner's permission to purchase something.

- It's a sign of weakness to ask for help.

- If I lose money, it isn't my fault, it's the economy or the advisor's.

These stereotypes and gender biases have been around for generations, but fortunately, they're starting to change.

Traditionally, women have seen money as a way to enjoy and enhance day-to-day life and create a lifestyle. In other words, it's all about the here and now.

Men, on the other hand, see money as something to be accumulated in order to gain value. It's all about the future. So, they typically don't spend–they invest.

As you can see, we have these pre-programmed, conditioned behaviours and stereotypes about money. Is it any wonder it can be so hard to sort this out in your relationship? We hardly know how to sort it out on our own.

Let's give it a go, shall we?

Now it's your turn. Go through each point in the stereotype list and the spending differences. Start with your parents and what you recall from their relationship with money. I am sure you will see a number of these behaviours in the earlier generations.

Then talk about what you have observed in your family history and see if any of them apply to you. You might even come up with some others.

CHAPTER 6

A NEW RELATIONSHIP - WHAT TO LOOK OUT FOR

A new relationship could be the first love, or it may be the second or third. If you were 'burned' financially in a previous relationship, you will be more cautious when entering the next one. But, as the saying goes, 'love is blind'. And when you are in the first flush of love, talking about money is probably the last thing on your mind, but you need to move it up the priority list.

When I spoke about money and mindset at a women's conference, it was plain that the topic of 'having the money conversation' was both compelling and troubling. I could see a few women shifting in their seats looking a little uncomfortable, so it wasn't too surprising that hands shot up when I finished speaking. The first question was this: 'My daughter is in a new relationship. When should she talk to the new boyfriend about money?'

'As soon as possible!' I said.

It's not something you do on a first or second date. But when you begin to move beyond the dating stage and a longer-term relationship looks likely, you need to have a conversation about money management.

Next question: 'Why do we need to do this?'

75

'Well', I replied, 'We come into each relationship with our own money beliefs and behaviours. Particularly if you have had money issues in the past, you bring that baggage with you and it needs to be dealt with or you'll repeat your mistakes'.

A healthy money marriage will have these conversations, uncomfortable as they might be.

What you want to achieve from the conversation is a framework that will work for you in the early phase of a relationship. It's usually about bill splitting and who will pay for what. There are many different 'rules' about whether the man should pay when you go out or whether you split the bill. Just make sure you sort out what is going to work best for you both.

If you have concerns about your partner's spending habits, now is a good time to discuss them. You also want to find out if your partner is carrying any debt, as in the future this could affect your future ability, either individually or jointly, to borrow money for something major. Again, timing is everything. You don't want to lose a potentially good relationship because you are being overzealous, so tread carefully.

One client asked me if she should get a credit check on a person she wanted to date. Personally, for me, that was a step too far, but I understood her anxiety. She had been left with debt from a previous relationship and didn't want to be in that situation again. She had changed her Money Personality from an Avoider to a Hoarder!

Look Out For Non-Negotiables

When we are in a new relationship, we have our rose-tinted glasses on, and the character traits we see in our new love are endearing. Even leaving the lid off the toothpaste is fine for the first few years! Once the rose-tinted glasses come off, some of those endearing traits become downright annoying. 'Will you put the lid on the toothpaste when you finish instead of letting it run all over the basin?' Many of these we can live with and adapt to if everything else in the relationship is going well. Let's face it, we all have our own character traits that drive our partner crazy too. Maybe yours is leaving your coffee mug in the sink instead of putting it in the dishwasher!

But when it comes to money, these character traits need to be talked about and worked through as the consequences can become much more serious over time.

If you fall in love with your polar money opposite, you will see money behaviours that make you uncomfortable, even in the early stages of your relationship when you are both on your 'best behaviour'. You need to be certain that you can live with these behaviours for the rest of your life. Can you discuss them early in your relationship before the differences become insurmountable?

How do you deal with this?

Start with watching your partner's behaviour with money. Do they seem reluctant to pick up the tab when you go out? Are they very generous with money? Do they seem to be obsessed with how much things cost, or very nonchalant?

As you observe this behaviour, think about how comfortable you are with it. Is that what you would do in the same situation? For example, how do you feel being with someone who bargains all the time or spends hours on the internet looking for the best deal? If you feel uncomfortable now, is it behaviour you will be able to tolerate long-term? Unless you are prepared to have the money conversation and resolve any issues, that behaviour isn't likely to change.

It isn't only your new partner's behaviour you need to think about. Yours needs some examination too. How does your partner respond to your money behaviour? You may need to be prepared to modify your habits.

Early in a relationship, you can identify the limits of your tolerance and decide if there are things that you just can't accept. Those at the top of the scale may persuade you to simply exit the relationship. Or if you feel the relationship is worth investing in, have the money conversation and get it out in the open. There is no guarantee anything will change, but it will help you understand if there is room for compromise and if the balance of positive factors in the relationship outweighs the money ones. Your partner may be wanting to have the money conversation too, so it could just as easily be the conversation that takes your relationship to the next level!

I was in my car listening to the radio while I was driving to a meeting. People were phoning in and giving reasons for ending relationships.

One woman phoned in to say she had been dating for a couple of months when her new man invited her to dinner at one of Auckland's best (and most expensive) restaurants. She was really excited and looking forward to the evening. It met all of her expectations of wonderful food and great service. At the end of the meal, when the bill was presented to her new man, he turned to her and asked her to pay for her half. The relationship died on the spot. Can you guess what his money personality was? Probably a Hoarder! She may well have been a Hoarder as well and just didn't appreciate half of the bill being sprung on her.

There were possibly other issues in the relationship and this was the one that made its demise inevitable. But it illustrates clearly the impact of discovering intolerable behaviour. After weighing other aspects of the relationship, she decided that continuing was out of the question.

Once you decide whether or not to continue with the relationship, you will have one of two conversations.

It might be the 'This isn't working sq we are through' conversation. On the other hand, it could be the 'Before we go any further in our relationship, there are a few things we need to talk about, and money is one of them.' You probably won't be as blunt as that, but I'm sure you get my drift. I've included in the workbook (http://www.moneymentalist.com/bookbonus) where you can find some examples of communication styles you can use to have money conversations with your partner.

Now it's your turn. Pull out your journal and jot down your recollections.

Think back to the early days when you were dating. Were there any niggly things you can recall about how each of you handled money? What about your circle of friends, what did you notice about their behaviour? You can already begin exploring the ways others have different money relationships through your friendships.

The second part of this is to notice if any of those early behaviours still niggle you, or do they make you smile? I don't want you to talk about these just yet—just be aware and journal about it so you can discuss it when you are ready.

CHAPTER 7

HOW DO YOU TALK ABOUT MONEY?

'Where do we start? What do we say?'

You've moved beyond the dating stage and things look serious. Longer-term plans are being made–you may be planning to move in together, open joint bank accounts, and move into the next phase of your relationship.

Or, maybe you've been together for several years and you still haven't gotten around to having a money conversation and things are starting to niggle you just a little.

If you haven't had the money conversation already, don't delay any further. You need to have a clear understanding of each other's relationship with money before you start combining finances and making joint financial decisions.

It's hard to gauge how big a part money plays in driving people apart, but it's pretty high on the list, along with sex. Lack of trust and communication are at the heart of both issues. Anecdotally, about 70-80% of relationships that break up blame money, and that is most often due to a lack of communication about it. This is evidenced in my divorce from Gaz, so I've experienced the impact firsthand.

When I mentioned this to a girlfriend over coffee, she was quite surprised. 'Bill and I talk about money all the time.'

There were a few seconds of silence while she bit at her scone. Then she added, 'No, you're right. We don't talk about money; we yell at each other about money.'

Why is this? Well, sometimes money arguments mask other issues within the relationship. This is because we attach emotions and meanings to money that has nothing to do with 1+1=2, as we discussed in Chapter 4.

So, if you are shouting at each other about money, listen very carefully for any underlying issues. According to Dr. John Gottman, some arguing is healthy, and about two-thirds of all arguments are perpetual. So, in five years, you will still be arguing about the same thing!

It isn't easy to take a step back in the heat of the moment. Once you have calmed down think back to how the argument started. How did it escalate? How did it go off the rails? At what point did it become about money? How did the argument end? If you see a common theme and pattern in each of your arguments, you are in a better position to be able to talk about them together and when they happen again, defuse them. It's the other 30% of arguments you really need to pay attention to. These are the ones that may well have deeper relationship issues, like power, control, and trust. Again, it's about unpacking them after the event when the heat of the moment has passed and the emotions have calmed down. Your and your partner's recollection of the argument may be quite different so be careful you don't start another one by trying to analyse the one you have just had!

I also work with couples who never argue about money; they just don't talk about it at all. These couples are very much in love, and the reason they don't talk about it is that they don't want to say something that could hurt or upset their partner. Conversations about spending too much or one partner not contributing enough to the finances are very difficult topics to raise so they simply sweep it under the carpet and hope that it will sort itself out over time.

Sometimes it does, but often it doesn't, and this is where resentment can start to kick in.

I didn't acknowledge how resentful I was becoming at the time. While I mostly wanted to protect my husband from my financial stress, to a degree I also blamed him because it didn't seem like was doing anything to make his situation *or* mine better. In his depression, he also stopped doing any maintenance around the property. So, not only was I drowning in my circumstances, I was now out there cutting trees and pruning on our huge property. I took on more and more while I observed Gaz just sitting there. Our money stories and personalities ran unrestrained while we swept our pain under the rug. It did not sort out over time–it imploded.

Additionally, many assumptions around our roles in the relationship can remain buried until some new issue erupts. Whether you've lost your job or won the lottery, tension will come bubbling to the surface. It may seem the argument is about money, but it may well be about who 'wears the pants', or how much or how little trust we have in the relationship, along with all the other emotions that are part of sharing your life with someone else.

This is where you can also talk about your different beliefs about money. For instance, maybe you are a Spender and believe that debt is fine. You don't care if you don't pay the credit card bill off each month. After all, money is there to be enjoyed! Your partner, on the other hand, maybe the thrifty type. She or he believes that money should be saved and not frittered away on 'stuff'. Such people have the mindset that if you don't have the money in the bank, you don't spend.

So, how do you resolve these differences so you can live in harmony? You have a money conversation.

If you feel you are in a good place in your relationship to have an in-depth money conversation, jump ahead to Part Three where you will find the guidelines. You will also find in Part Three the Money Dump exercise which is designed to help you release all of your frustrations (and the good things as well) about how you and your partner currently work together with your money.

If you feel you aren't quite there yet, that's fine too. Keep reading and doing the exercises from Part One. Once you are clear about your relationship with money you will find it easier to engage with your partner about money.

Head to www.moneymentalist.com/bookbonus for the bonus workbook and exclusive readers free gifts for more resources.

CHAPTER 8

OUR MONEY PERSONALITIES
ARE DIFFERENT!

In Chapter 1 I introduced the concept of your money personality. If you still don't know yours, go to www.moneymentalist.com and take the quiz. Ask your partner to do the quiz as well, then compare your results and see how similar or different you are.

The Money Personality styles that I talk about were developed by Olivia Mellan (now retired), so when we look at how your style and your partner's style can fit together, I am referring to Olivia's work in this area.

I am sure you have looked at couples around and wondered to yourself, *How on earth did they get together? They are so different.* We all know that opposites attract and that may apply when you look at your own relationship.

Even if you don't start as opposites, you quite often end up that way. For example, if two Spenders get together, they will vie for the 'Master Spender' role and the loser will end up taking on hoarding characteristics–someone has to be sensible and pay the bills! The same applies if two Hoarders get together; they will fight each other to be 'Super Hoarder' but once the cupboards are bare and the electricity has been cut off, one of them has to become the Spender (even if only at a very low level).

Opposites attract can also apply to our money personality. Polarisation occurs when you are the direct opposite of your partner, an introvert and an extrovert, for example, one wants to stay home and the other wants to go out and party.

Over time these polarisations (both in life and with money) can become more rigid and lead to conflict. Each partner starts to attack the other. The introvert accuses the extrovert of never being home, leaving them to take on a greater share of responsibility for the home. The extrovert accuses the introvert of being boring and not wanting to do anything. You can see the slippery slope here.

Over time, through the eyes of the Spender, their Hoarder partner is a cheapskate and obsessed with money! The Hoarder is worried that their Spender partner will send them broke, leave them in debt, and they'll have nothing to retire on. Frustration builds as more and more 'stuff' arrives home after shopping expeditions.

Let's explore some of these polarisations.

Common Money personality Pairings

Spender and Hoarder

Just a quick recap on your money personality. If you are a Spender, it's all about instant gratification and immediate pleasure, spend it now and worry about tomorrow later. You enjoy spending your money. Budget? What budget? I don't need to save—I can use my credit card. You find it easy to overspend, which can result in debt.

If you're paired with a Hoarder personality, you're living with your polar opposite. For them, saving money is important, as is having financial goals. Hoarders want to budget and plan their spending, and they find it hard to spend money on the good things in life. They are very good at delaying gratification and prioritising their spending.

The stereotype is that the woman is the Spender and the man is the Hoarder. In reality, there is no gender bias here at all. So, you can't use that as an excuse for your behaviour!

This pairing finds it very easy to argue about money; the blame game of 'you spend too much' and 'you are tight' is very easy to latch onto. But when this pairing gets over the arguing about who did (or didn't do) what, they are a very powerful combination.

When they work in harmony together they make very good decisions by meeting in the middle. They can see both sides of what they want to achieve and can decide the best approach to take, save for what they want or go ahead and spend.

Here's a story that can help you see how the Spender/Hoarder partnership can get along.

The guest bathroom was looking old and tired. It had been 'put up with' for several years but the time had come to renovate and tidy it up. The happy Spender was all set to bring in the builders–the plumber, the painter, and every other trade required, and it was off to the closest bathroom shop (which also happened to be the most expensive in town) to pick the fittings. *Let's just get this done*, was the attitude.

The careful Hoarder, on the other hand, looked at the job and thought to themselves, *How much of this project can we do ourselves?* They were happy to research the fittings online and come up with a shortlist for the Spender to look at. Quality was important but so was getting a good deal.

The happy Spender was worried the job would never get finished if they did it themselves, so a timeframe was put in place, and if it wasn't complete by that date, the builders would be coming. This gave our careful Hoarder a very good incentive to do their part.

The result was a new bathroom that met both partners' requirements and it was achieved without breaking the bank or looking 'cheap'. A great outcome was completed on time and within budget!

You can see how this can work in a project situation, but how do you resolve the difference in day-to-day life? Recognise that there are no rights or wrongs in each of the styles, there are strengths in each that you need to tap into to work as a team. The way you do this is to acknowledge to each other what you appreciate about the other's style. The Hoarder, for example, may appreciate that their Spender partner has created a relaxing environment at home by adding little touches here and there. The Spender may appreciate that their Hoarder partner is looking after their future security by saving for retirement.

This sounds straightforward, doesn't it? The reason it isn't is fear. The Hoarder is worried that if they say to their Spender partner that they love the 'little touches' at home, that will give the Spender licence to spend even more. And the Spender is worried that if they say to their Hoarder partner that they are grateful they are saving for retirement, the purse strings will get tightened even more.

Once you stop attacking the behaviour and look at the underlying reasons why you behave the way you do, then you can more easily agree on how to work with your differences. Remember, as I talked about in Part One, our behaviours come from our beliefs, which come from our environment, so this is a perfect opportunity to have a money conversation about what it was like growing up in your family or previous relationships.

Now it's your turn. Spend a day in each other's shoes... take some time out and go shopping. The Hoarder **has** to spend money on themselves and the Spender can't spend money at all. This will help as you observe each other's behaviour and how it feels when the shoe is on the other foot.

Debrief when you get home. How did it feel to be in each other's shoes? What did you observe in each other as you watched your partner be you?

Amasser and Money Monk

This pairing is not only polarizing in terms of money, but can also polarize in terms of values, beliefs, and philosophy as well. This also means this is a very dynamic couple.

Let's do a quick recap of the personality style of each. A traditional Money Monk believes that money is bad; they feel uncomfortable if they have money, and are very aware of the needs of others. A more modern Money Monk doesn't necessarily believe money is bad, but they are still uncomfortable having too much of it. They have a very strong social conscious about how they spend their money.

On the other hand, the Amasser believes that money equals power/self-worth (in a good way most of the time). They believe their life will be better the more money that they have.

You can see how this pairing is dynamic but can also be fraught with tension, looking at the world from two completely different perspectives.

When I meet a couple with this pairing, I always ask what brought them together in the first place. This causes them to reflect on the parts of each other that they admired and that they have possibly lost sight of over time. Refocusing on that can help bring the polarization closer together.

I often hear from the Amasser, 'I love that he/she wasn't tied down by mortgages, had the freedom to go places and do things, and just get by on what they had'. The Money Monk often loved that their Amasser partner was driven and going places.

As with our Spender-Hoarder pairing, looking at the strengths of each style and what you admire about each style will be the turning point of making this partnership work.

The Amasser can use the wealth they create to support the Money Monk in causes that are close to their heart. The Money Monk may be in a position where they don't have to earn their income, they can donate their time to causes and charities that need help. And the Money Monk can work with the Amasser to invest their money in ethical, environmentally sound investments, for example.

It's also about communicating with each other about your underlying beliefs and how they came about so you can understand each other's viewpoints more clearly.

Now it's your turn. If this polarization is causing you some issues in your relationship then work together to look for examples that debunk your own biases and views of the world. There will be Money Monks who have created wealth purely to give it away and still live a very humble lifestyle. Just as there will be Amassers who lead happy and full lives knowing they have made more than enough in their careers, have everything they could ever want, and plan to give away large portions of their wealth to help others.

Avoiders And The Other Personality Types

I often refer to Avoiders as my problem child... Avoiders are the highest risk personality style to be financially abused or taken advantage of by their partner (in both business and life).

Avoiders avoid looking at their money; they often don't know what comes in and where it goes. They may feel incompetent and not able to manage money, so they don't try.

In a relationship, they will happily delegate all financial responsibility to their partner–sometimes to the point of delegation by abdication where they won't even engage in conversation with their partner about money.

You can see how this can cause stress from several different aspects.

If you pick the wrong partner, you can find yourself in dire financial straits should the relationship end. 'I trusted you to look after me and our money, what happened?' is often asked after the fact when the lawyers are working out who gets what.

If you have a loving partner, you are putting a lot of stress on them to manage the finances single-handedly. This is made even more difficult if the Avoider won't even engage in a discussion about money. As long as the credit card works, they are happy. So, when stuff happens, as it does in life, the loving partner is left to sort it out, then get blamed if it doesn't work out well.

If you have this pairing, then it's very difficult to break out of it, as quite often the Avoider is resistant to discussing the situation and then making the necessary changes.

Now it's your turn. It's up to the partner who isn't the Avoider to instigate some small actions to gently guide their Avoider partner. Maybe leave a bank statement on the table (you will probably have to print it from your online banking first). Start engaging in low-level financial chit-chat about friends, for example, 'John mentioned that his power bill has jumped up this winter, so I had a look at ours, and I noticed the same thing". Leave it at that for now and build slowly from there.

How Can You Resolve Your Polarization?

As with all the other polarizations, communication and understanding why this personality style is dominant in you or your partner is the key to shifting to a better position.

Here are the five steps to successful depolarization:

1. Communicate openly and honestly with your partner.

2. Acknowledge what you secretly admire and envy about their money personality.

3. Learn to 'move towards the middle' by practising behaviours and attitudes that don't come naturally to you.

4. Monitor and record your reactions to the new behaviours.

5. Reward yourself for your successes—but not by resorting to your old behaviours.

Depolarizing doesn't mean that the Hoarder has become a Spender or vice versa, it simply means that you understand and can deal with the tension between the different styles. You have moved to the middle ground.

Empathy and respect for your partner's strengths and weaknesses will help you achieve this.

But as we all know, and as Forrest Gump so aptly put it, 'Life is like a box of chocolates. You never know what your gonna get'. So sometimes your money conversations will be plain sailing and go really well, and sometimes you may well find yourself heading into an argument.

CHAPTER 9

ARGUMENTS ARE INEVITABLE, PARTICULARLY WHEN IT COMES TO MONEY!

'You are screwing with my life'! is not the best way to start any conversation, let alone one about money with your partner.

Unfortunately, that is how a lot of conversations between partners end up if one is feeling frustrated and angry at the lack of communication about money in the relationship.

'I thought I was doing the right thing by supporting my wife and family so she didn't have to go to work', is what one husband said after his marriage of 25 years ended. It turns out, that wasn't what his wife wantcd. She wanted to be more self-sufficient and financially independent within the relationship, but neither of them knew how to talk about what they wanted or what the other thought until it was too late.

'I had no idea what was going on with our finances. I thought we were doing okay, there were no boundaries around my spending; he never told me if I was spending too much.' This was from a wife whose husband ended the relationship and through the process of splitting their assets, found out things weren't as rosy as she thought.

Or consider my situation... I was $600,000 in debt after Gaz and I parted ways. Even I didn't realize how bad it was until the end. I thought I was doing the right thing by sparing him from the details, as stressed as he already was. Imagine his stress had he known how in debt I was!

Stress and arguing over money in the relationship is a bad sign, but it worsens if you never discuss it at all. Sadly, many of us have inherited money habits or behaviours that weaken our financial security and our closest relationships.

This happens in a lot of relationships because many of us were raised in homes where money was a taboo subject.

Money might be difficult to talk about, but it's very easy to argue about. It arouses emotions easily and can mask other issues in the relationship. You may say, 'We never argue about money'. In some ways, that's just as difficult as arguing about it. Why?

As I touched on in Chapter 7, there are two ends to the spectrum. At one end are the couples who are very vocal and yell, argue, debate, and have robust conversations about money. Sometimes the arguments are about money, in which case when you sort out the money issue, the arguments go away, and the relationship is back on track. However, sometimes the money arguments are masking deeper issues within the relationship, so working on the money may not resolve the arguing, and in some cases, the relationship ends once the money is 'fixed' and everything else is exposed.

At the other end of the spectrum are couples who don't really talk about money. They think they are, but the conversations are transactional. 'Gosh, the price of petrol has gone up again. We'll need to cut back on the lunches, or maybe we can carpool to stay on track', or 'I need to go shopping as Jonny needs new shoes for school, how much have we got in the kitty for this?' They aren't the important money conversations like 'Are we financially okay right now?' or 'What are our long-term plans for financial security?' etc. Often the reason the conversations aren't happening is that one partner doesn't want to hurt the other. Having a conversation that goes along the lines of 'We aren't financially okay right now because you aren't taking responsibility for your spending' isn't easy.

Here are some of the most common topics that couples argue about when it comes to money. Some of these topics we have already covered, but now we'll explore them in the context of relationships.

Now it's your turn. As you read the list of reasons that couples argue about money, write down which of them (if any) apply to you and your partner. If you don't argue about money, write about why you think that might be.

Common Money Arguments

Different money personalities

You know all about this one. This will often come across as 'You're spending too much', or 'You're too tight'. You know from the previous chapter that opposites attract, and instead of looking at your money personalities as something to argue about, look for the strengths of each personality style. Remember your Money Personality is a behaviour style, but in the heat of an argument, it's easy to attack your partner and not just the behaviour. If this is you, go back to the money conversation, role play, and talk about what your parents were like with money, in other words, drill back down into the money beliefs that you each have, as that is where your differences come from.

Different beliefs and values

We spent the whole of Part One talking about your money beliefs. When you come together in a relationship, you need to understand each other's money beliefs.

As I have said, just as we don't talk about our relationship with money with each other, I also don't know too many couples who sit down at breakfast one morning and look each other lovingly in the eyes and say, 'Honey, let's talk about our money beliefs'. But maybe we should... it would save a whole heap of arguments in the future. You are going to be equipped to do this by having the money conversation and also doing the work on your relationship with money so that you are clear about your own beliefs and values when you have the conversation with your partner.

Who controls the money?

This is a difficult one, as often an underlying power and control issue is going on. Whoever controls the money can often control the relationship, particularly if one partner is dependent on the other for providing the bulk of the household income. Signs to look out for here are that your partner expects to have access to all of your bank accounts, but not the other way around. Or, if you have joint accounts, you are given an allowance and don't see any of the other transactions. This type of behaviour can creep up on you over time. It may have initially seemed like a great idea. If left unchecked, at the extreme end, it can become financial abuse. By the time you realise what's going on, it can be difficult to turn things around, as the power and control may be showing up in other areas of your relationship as well.

The flip side to this is when one partner completely abdicates responsibility to the other and won't enter into a discussion about money, even if their partner wants to (think about the

Avoider Personality here). This leaves their partner in the stressful situation of having the money management dropped on them and they may not feel equipped to handle it. They may try to engage in a money conversation and get rebutted, often in a loving way. Frustration can grow as well as stress and this is when the arguments begin. The best way to address this is to have a conversation that isn't initially about money. It might be that you start engaging your partner about money by talking about the next family holiday—ask them to do some research so they start to see what things cost. Ask for multiple options. That way you can ease the conversation towards affordability if that is a concern for you.

In some pairings, tough love is required and you just have to let the card get declined, though be careful here that your credit rating doesn't get impacted.

No goals or plans

In that first flush of love, we have dreams, we have places we want to go, and things we want to do. Then we get into the routine of day-to-day living and can easily let those dreams drift away. But what if one of you is happy to drift along and enjoy the here and now, while the other wants to plan for the future, the holiday, the house, and the family? It's a balancing act; you need to learn how to save for the things you want as well as live for the now... this is a skill that many couples don't master, instead they remain frustrated and angry with each other, and it becomes a bone of contention. A niggle in their relationship. As you mature, the no plans and goals can become a concern about future security and retirement.

What many families do to live in the here and now and to have what they want is to borrow money, and that leads us to the next round of arguing. One of the ways to avoid this is to have some separate money, so the partner who wants to save can do so. I was presenting at a workshop and one of the attendees did exactly this. She and her Spender husband had their own 'free money accounts'. She used hers as a savings account and invested the money. He spent his. They didn't argue about it, as the money was theirs to do with what they wanted. While this was a creative solution, this couple did break up after about 15 years together. The lack of working together towards their future became too much for her and she decided to leave the relationship.

Look at this as a short-term solution. The long-term one is to spend time together talking about what the shared vision for your relationship is. There are often goals, but they might be on different timeframes. Unless you talk about them you will continue to sabotage each other.

Debt

One of you is comfortable with debt, the other isn't. This argument stems from your beliefs about debt and your upbringing or early environment and how you saw debt within your family. It can also stem from the fear of having too much debt, not being able to pay it back, and losing everything. Arguments can also arise because one of you 'forgot' to mention some debt that you brought into the relationship. The longer you stay silent, the harder it becomes to talk about it. I've heard many stories from mortgage brokers who have been in situations where a couple is sitting in their office and a debt pops up that one of the partners knew nothing about!

I've had similar experiences in my days as an accountant. Once I was having my first cup of tea for the day and reviewing my diary to see who was coming to see me when my heart sank. Some meetings you know are going to be difficult and I had one of those scheduled for the afternoon.

Bruce was coming to see me. He was in a bit of a pickle. He had been in business for five years, had never prepared financial statements, and had never paid any tax. He had managed to slip under the radar of the tax department, but the worry about how much he might owe was starting to eat him up.

His tax bill, we calculated, was around $100,000; all the penalties and interest would, at a minimum, probably double his debt. He took it as well as could be expected. At least it was now a real number and he felt he could deal with it. The problem was he hadn't told his wife any of this. They had been married a couple of years and he never quite got around to telling her. She was completely in the dark, and it was my obligation to tell her if he wouldn't. Hence, the afternoon meeting.

The meeting room was prepared—water, coffee, biscuits, tissues—and I waited for the couple to arrive. It was the first time I had met Karen. I could see she was a little apprehensive as to why she had to be there.

It wasn't long before we got down to business.

'Karen', I said, 'there's no easy way to break this to you. Bruce got behind in his tax obligations and at this point he owes the tax department approximately $100,000.' Before I could continue, she broke down in tears.

Once she calmed down, she looked across the table at Bruce. 'Honey,' she said, 'it isn't the tax I'm worried about. It's the $50,000 credit card debt I have that I've never told you about'.

There was stunned silence. This was a couple in major financial strife, and neither had dared to talk to the other about it. *What else*, I wondered, *is bubbling below the surface?*

The best way to address situations like this is to have a neutral third party (Financial Therapist, Money Mentor/coach) in the room. They can help keep emotions in check and manage the conversation in a non-emotional and non-judgmental way.

This story does have a happy conclusion. This meeting revealed a whole raft of other issues in their relationship, which they chose to address by seeing a couple's counsellor. They sorted out their debt by selling their house and all the surplus 'stuff' they had acquired and scrutinised everything about their lifestyle. The last I heard of them they were very happy parents of a baby boy.

Joint or Separate Accounts

This issue can cause a lot of grief, usually because merging or not merging hasn't been thought through enough. We deep dive into this when we get practical in Part Three.

Keeping financial secrets (financial infidelity)

Of all the arguments, this is the hardest one for a relationship to recover from. It's a major breach of trust in your relationship and can kill it. This is such an important topic that the next chapter will cover it in much more detail.

How is your list looking? Are you seeing a common theme or are your arguments more random?

The Negative Impact of Arguing About Money

There are many money topics that you can argue about. They are typically subsets of the major topics listed above. For example, arguing about pocket money for children stems from differing beliefs and values.

It may come as a surprise that arguing is okay and it can be productive. It's part of being in a committed relationship. In fact, it's a red flag according to Dr John Gottman, if couples *don't* argue!

There are healthy ways to argue and there are unhealthy ways to argue (in the workbook (www.moneymentalist.com/bookbonus) you will find links to Dr John Gottman's advice). It's the unhealthy continuous unresolved arguing about money that can have some very serious impacts on your relationship, in more areas than just financially.

Couples who say their relationship is just okay often don't talk about their dreams or plans. They avoid talking about the money aspect of how to achieve them, so they lack focus and direction. It's easy to just drift out of a relationship that is just floating along.

Too much stress, whether it's financial or in any other aspect of your life, impacts your health—you don't sleep, you might get aches and pains, and you are constantly feeling a bit anxious. This type of stress isn't good long-term and something will give. Often it's the relationship that pays the price.

Where money is a constant source of tension, financial anxiety can set in, and you start to doubt your own ability to make sound financial decisions. You doubt your partner, you feel unsupported, and this can lead to a lack of trust and communication. This can in turn lead to financial infidelity, which as I mentioned before is a very slippery slope indeed. The most extreme case of this I have seen is one where the husband's business was struggling, so rather than talking to his wife about how they could work together to resolve this, he borrowed against the family home on more than one occasion. The business continued to decline and the first the wife knew about the family home being at risk was when the bank phoned to say the house was going to a mortgagee sale! She knew her husband was worried about money but didn't know to what extent. She chose to continue to support him despite losing the family home and did so for another couple of years. But at the end of the day, they couldn't rebuild the trust that had been broken and they went their separate ways.

You have heard this numerous times now, but it is good to keep it top of mind. Anecdotally, 70-80% of relationships that break up blame money.

There *is* light at the end of the tunnel. Many of these money arguments can be resolved with a bit of help and support. And of course, being prepared to do the work to solve the arguments for good.

So, if money is an ongoing issue in your relationship, how do you resolve it?

Here are seven things you can do to resolve your money arguments:

1. **Have 'the money conversation':** This is set out for you in Part Three. If you are in a new relationship, have it sooner rather than later. While your first date might be a bit early, as soon as things start getting serious it's an important consideration. If money is causing friction in your relationship at any stage, face the issue head-on. While the initial conversations may be tough or awkward, the sooner you and your partner can get on the same financial page, the more relationship satisfaction you'll have.

   If you are already in a long-term relationship, you can still have the conversation. You have to be careful that it doesn't turn into a blame game and that it's constructive. Included in the bonuses are some different communication tools to help you have a money conversation. It can be hard to break out of your usual patterns of behaviour so trying something different can help. Once you get into the swing of having money conversations turn them into regular date nights.

2. **Understand that you will have different beliefs and values about money:** You may have been raised by thrifty parents, while your partner's might have been Spenders. Recognise that you will each have different beliefs and that there is no one right way to manage your money. Sharing money stories from your past helps identify what some of these beliefs are. Your early memories are a great starting point.

3. **Plan for big life changes:** If money is a pressure point at the start of your relationship, adding a mortgage or kids is bound to create more stress. Before you make a decision with a big financial impact, figure out what the change will mean for your finances and how your spending habits will need to adapt.

4. **Keep talking (not shouting!):** Bottling up your frustration at another big credit card bill, or hitting the roof when the statement arrives, is not going to resolve the issue. Going on an attack about your partner's financial habits will make them defensive, so make an effort to talk calmly and rationally.

5. **Get help and advice from a qualified third party, like a Financial Therapist or Money Mentor/ coach:** Sometimes it's just too hard to communicate rationally about money. If this is the case in your relationship, the unbiased advice of a third party will be invaluable. While friends are great, it can be hard for them to be unbiased, plus they have their own Money Stories going on, so it's best to use a qualified Financial Therapist or Money coach. They can help you and your partner understand one another's perspectives, identify

joint financial priorities, and learn to work together to achieve them. If your relationship needs more support then couples counselling is a good option as well.

6. **Have a shared bank account.** Even if you don't want to fully merge your finances, having a joint bank account that you both contribute to, with clear guidelines about what the account is for, will help build money trust between you.

7. **Keep the end in mind and don't be afraid to compromise.** You came together as a couple because you loved each other and wanted to spend the rest of your lives together. Don't let money get in the way of that. Instead, plan how you can use your money to achieve the dreams and goals that you have. Money is just a tool to help you get there. And yes, we all need to compromise at some time or other, but if you have a shared vision for where you want your relationship to go, compromise becomes easier.

Whatever stage your relationship is in, it's important to remember that working together–not against each other–will ensure a brighter financial future for you both.

Understanding what the vision is for your relationship, being on the same page financially, and going in the same direction at the same time makes a very powerful combination. Wrapping your values around that makes you unstoppable!

I can't help but look back and think to myself, *I wish I could turn back time.* We are just expected to know this money stuff. If you were fortunate enough to come from a family background where it just worked between your parents, you had a huge head start on figuring it out in your relationship. Gaz and I, like you, are intelligent, had good careers, and were very capable in our roles that generated the income. But when it came to what we did with it, that's a very different story.

Gaz and I fell into the 'we don't argue about money' camp. We didn't discuss it either. I do recall one time when we had just come back from a holiday in Thailand (it had been a stressful trip due to a fairly major incident with one of my accounting clients). We had dropped my daughter at her dad's and were driving home. I don't know how the discussion started but Gaz was angry and said something like, 'I spent the last of my money on this trip, and you were running around buying jewellery'! I was stunned for a couple of reasons. First of all, Gaz didn't get angry often, and it was the first I knew that he (and his business) had run out of money.

What was going on beneath the surface of this sentence? Even then it didn't turn into a conversation! I was happily living out of my own belief and money story that I could have whatever I wanted, whenever I wanted it, whether I could afford it or not. (I still have the piece of jewellery by the way). Gaz was living out his belief and money story that he needed to be the provider, so said yes to the trip, even though he was concerned about money. Had we communicated we probably wouldn't have taken the trip.

Because we didn't have the money conversation, we never discussed our money beliefs. We thought we knew each other's money stories from our past relationships but never connected them to how they would flow into our relationship. We didn't plan or have a vision for our relationship. Like many couples, we were living in the moment, which is fine, until it all goes wrong.

CHAPTER 10

FINANCIAL INFIDELITY - WHAT IS IT AND HOW IT CAN DESTROY YOUR RELATIONSHIP

Is financial infidelity as destructive to your relationship as a sexual affair? When a local radio station polled listeners on this very question the response was about 50/50. The reality is, both can damage a relationship beyond repair, as they are major breaches of trust. But with financial infidelity, you have the financial fallout to deal with which can take years to recover from, whether you remain together or not.

Financial infidelity can seem harmless enough, buying something that you know you shouldn't and hiding it away. You bring it out saying breezily, 'I've had this for ages'. Both men and women do this. For many couples, financial infidelity only goes that far. But for others, it can escalate to real financial harm and relationship breakdown.

What Is Financial Infidelity?

It is making and then hiding financial decisions when you are in a relationship. It isn't just the making of the decision or even the hiding of it. It's the two together that breach the trust and when infidelity occurs.

As with any infidelity, it's the breach of trust that is the hardest part to work through and get over.

What Are The Signs?

What do we look for to see whether there is financial infidelity?

It starts small, as things just pop out of the wardrobe or the garden shed.

Or you might question your partner. 'Oh, I love the new sunglasses. How much were they?' And they reply, 'They were only $150'. And then you see them advertised on Google and they're $600. You'll probably let it go, assuming they were on sale, or you might ask more questions and get slightly terse answers. If this becomes a pattern of behaviour, your suspicions will be aroused about what is really going on.

Financial infidelity is easier to hide if couples don't have merged finances. You might have set up a 'bills' account where you contribute jointly to pay the household expenses, and whatever is left over is yours. In this situation, the 'it's my money, I'll do what I like' attitude comes into play.

If you have had the money conversation and discussed how your finances are going to work in practice, then it's not financial infidelity if you don't disclose everything. But often the 'bills' account is a bit random, there's no clarity about what is joint and what isn't and who pays for anything other than bills. Typically, one partner ends up bearing more of the brunt for the 'other' expenses and resentment builds up and that can lead to financial infidelity.

Common Examples Of Financial Infidelity:

A secret credit card that your partner knows nothing about. It's very easy to get credit, so it's also easy to get a credit card in your own name without telling your partner if you don't want to. The thought process here often starts quite innocently.

Maybe there's a special event coming up and you don't have quite enough money, so you put it on your new card, certain you will be able to pay it off by the due date. But what if you can't? What if you continue to use it and wrack up debt that your partner doesn't know anything about? If you are managing the payments, I can hear you say, 'So what?' Let's take this one step further: you and your partner want to buy your first home together and you are sitting in the bank or with your broker going through the list of what you owe so they can work out how much you can borrow. Probably not the best time to have to disclose your secret card—it's embarrassing for you and it's *very* awkward for the banker or broker. But it's a lot more common than you think.

Inflating the weekly grocery spend by withdrawing cash to buy yourself 'stuff' that your partner doesn't know about. This behaviour often stems from the feeling that you are being controlled or you don't have any money of your own and don't feel that you can ask for it. I see this behaviour in situations where the relationship is already in trouble and the 'skimming' is going on due to fear of financial support ending once the relationship does.

Continuing to financially support an ex-partner without telling your current partner. This is a tricky one. You may still feel some responsibility (often through guilt) for your ex-partner. You are torn between helping them and telling your current partner and potentially creating an argument with them. It's best to talk to your current partner before helping your ex. Yes, the conversation may not be easy, but it's much better to have it beforehand than for your partner to find out later. Again, it comes down to why you feel the need to support your ex, how much that support is, and what impact it's having on your current relationship.

Not disclosing your total income to your partner. This is more common when the finances are separate, and your income is going into a personal rather than a joint account. I had an initial meeting with a potential client who wanted me to help with not only her business but also the couple's finances as well. Her husband wasn't at the initial meeting, and I never got to meet him in person, but I did have a very interesting phone conversation with him. He called me and very aggressively told me that he was only prepared to disclose a certain amount of his income to his wife, anything else that he earned was his to do with as he wanted and that was that. I went back to his wife and said that I could continue to work with her and her business, but as her husband did not want to engage in the process of the couple's finances, I couldn't help them. About a year later, she was in the middle of a very messy divorce. She discovered he was having an affair. Once he was found out, the aggression he'd directed towards me came out in full force at her!

Racking up debt to cover a gambling (or some other) addiction. I think this is probably the saddest form of financial infidelity as it comes from a place of addiction. You may still love each other and want to save the relationship but unless the addiction is dealt with the financial aspect is always going to be a struggle. It takes a very strong couple to come out the other side of this.

Where the line is for you comes down to your values. Many of us only learn what our values are when confronted with something that challenges us. This is true with our financial comforts as well. When we find ourselves challenged in these situations, it's helpful to ask ourselves: Where on the financial infidelity scale is this? Can my relationship survive it?

What Causes Financial Infidelity?

- You may be concerned about family finances and want to 'tuck money away' just in case.

- You're unsure about the relationship and want an 'escape fund'. There are times when I have recommended this course of action to a client. It isn't something that I generally condone, but there are circumstances where you may need to do this.

  o If you have no income and are going to be totally reliant on your ex-partner initially for income after the split.

  o If you're concerned that access to funds will be cut off for you (and often the children) to control the outcome of the separation.

In these circumstances, if you can build a cash reserve you could have some peace of mind from worrying about the day-to-day finances, so you can focus on other issues.

- You might feel that your partner is too controlling with the money. This can happen when we have polar opposite money personalities—the Spender feels they are being controlled by their partner who has the purse strings. They don't want to have to keep asking for money or face questions when they spend from the joint account, so to solve this problem they will open a secret bank account or credit card and happily spend. Their Hoarder partner can be doing the same thing, but with a different motivation. They want to tuck money away so they don't go broke!

Financial control for power is more insidious. This is deliberate control by the partner who earns the money to maintain power in the relationship by saying yes or no to the other one who isn't earning.

It can also arise from a feeling of entitlement. 'It's my money, I'll spend it how I want.' This is about power and control and not feeling the need to share financial decisions with your partner.

Sometimes you might not even be aware that you are committing financial infidelity.

Consider this scenario:

Your teenager, Sam, has spent all his allowance and despite knowing the bank of Mum and Dad is closed, really wants to head out with friends. Sam decides, as teenagers do, to wheedle the money out of Mum. On this day, however, Mum is feeling strong and says no.

So, Sam goes to Dad, who is tired at the end of the day and for the sake of peace, hands Sam the cash and jokingly says, 'Just don't tell Mum'.

Sam happily heads out with friends leaving Mum and Dad at home. A bit later in the evening, Mum says to Dad, 'Did you give Sam some money?'

At this point, Dad has two choices.

1. Come clean and confess it was him and put up with a growling from his wife, or

2. Tell a little white lie and say it wasn't him and that maybe Sam borrowed the money from a mate.

If Dad chooses option 2, that is financial infidelity.

I can hear you all saying, 'So what!? We do this all the time.' And you're right, in the scheme of things, this is low on the financial infidelity scale.

But what message is Sam getting? If this only happens once or twice it isn't likely to have much impact on him.

But consider the situation where the children are constantly hearing from both sides, 'Don't tell Mum' or 'Don't tell Dad'. That can have serious ramifications for them as they enter their own relationships. This is becoming a much more common scenario for children where their parents split up.

They may enter a relationship with the belief that it's normal to hide money and things from their partner. This could lead them to believe that it's typical behaviour to have secret credit cards or money tucked away in secret bank accounts.

How Do You Nip Financial Infidelity In The Bud?

Here are five things you can do: We will do a deep dive into each of these in Part Three. Plus you can find additional resources here www.moneymentalist.com/bookbonus.

1. **Have the money conversation** early in your relationship. You will have heard me talk about the money conversation several times by now. I cannot stress just how important this is. You need to establish some financial boundaries. Talk about different scenarios and how you feel about them. For example, is there a limit that you can lend money to friends and family without discussing it first? What levels of debt and savings are you bringing to the relationship? What are your financial expectations?

2. **Have a household banker.** This is the person who is responsible for managing the household finances. They

make sure all the bills get paid, the savings plan is implemented, and your financial goals are reached. You can swap this role around; it doesn't always have to be the same person.

3. **Don't delegate your financial responsibilities totally to your partner.** You may not be 'good with money', but you still need to know what's going on and have access to joint bank accounts and credit cards for example.

4. **Have your own money.** It's important that each of you have your own money that doesn't have to be accounted for. This can be any amount that you agree upon. It could be as little as $25 a week or $1,000, it really depends on your financial circumstances. By having your own money, you may not feel the need to hide purchases or feel guilty if you indulge yourself a little.

5. **Take financial date nights.** Have regular financial date nights where you talk about your finances. Are you on track to meet your long-term financial goals? How are you doing compared to your Money Plan? What are some short-term savings goals you are working towards?

If you are concerned that financial infidelity may be going on, you need to deal with it sooner rather than later. Talk to your partner, not in an accusing argumentative state; although it's very difficult to not get emotional about your finances. If you feel you can't raise it yourself, get some help from a Financial Therapist or Money Mentor/Coach who can help you have the conversation and deal with the consequences.

As with any type of infidelity, the main point is to not let it fester. The sooner you deal with financial infidelity the better and the less financial harm you may suffer.

If your relationship is strong, with good communication and some processes in place for the future, you will make it out to the other side.

Let's keep working through other facets of how to have a happy money relationship in marriage!

CHAPTER 11

HOW TO HAVE A HAPPY MONEY MARRIAGE

We have covered quite a lot of trouble spots and what to look for when you fall in love and want to merge, not only your lives, but your relationships with money as well. It may seem that there are more negatives than positives. Let me assure you that this isn't the case.

A lot of couples have no problems at all blending their relationships with money together; it comes naturally to them. Others have to work at it. Guess what? The work is worth it. For all that Gaz and I suffered in silence trying to protect the other— I would trade it in a heartbeat for the hard, uncomfortable confessions of our financial failures and fears.

A happy money marriage is a key ingredient to a happy relationship. We all want a life happily ever after with the person of our dreams. But the sad reality is... here's that statistic again: 70% – 80% of relationships that break up blame money.

So, if you want a happy money marriage you need to talk about money regularly and deal with money as a couple.

Key Ingredients To A Happy Money Marriage:

Communicate, communicate, communicate about money

As I have said often, communication is not yelling at each other or saying nothing. It's having a conversation with each other, listening to each, and talking to each other.

You now know how to speak your money language. You can openly discuss the good, the bad, and the ugly about your finances. You know and understand each other's financial baggage.

Some of the conversations are quite straightforward and quite transactional and easy to have. Others are more difficult as they relate to your beliefs and values and these are the ones that can cause stress.

Have regular financial date nights (or lunch or breakfast). I give you the agenda and outline for this in Part Three. This is the time you set aside to have the money conversations. You will talk about the transactional stuff and cover how you are tracking against your Money Plan, what needs to be tweaked, what was unexpected, and most importantly, share the wins. Date nights are also a great opportunity to plan and look forward to the future; this is the most exciting part of your date nights. You will talk about how to look after your money together, nurture it together, and plan for it together. This is all about planning the future, weekends away, and holidays. Do you want to buy a house? Do you want to have extended time away? You are jointly and actively working together as a team to decide what you are going to do with your money and do it regularly.

Have a shared vision for your relationship

I don't just mean financial, this is about your life together—what you want to do, where you want to go, and what you want to achieve together as a couple. In our busy lives, we often never get around to talking about this. This is a vision, so it can change as your relationship matures. Your vision will form the basis for your goals. We often want the same things, but we might be working toward them in different time frames. For example, you might want to travel and then start a family. Your partner might want to buy a house and then travel. Travel is there for both of you, but the order and timing are different. Once you have identified the timing difference, use your financial date nights to talk about it and prioritise what is going to work best for you.

Have joint goals, both short and long-term

When you were in the early phase of your relationship you probably talked about the dreams that you had, the travel you wanted to do, and maybe owning your home. It is now time to get serious about turning those dreams into goals together and working towards them. You don't want to wake up in 20 years and realise they have all slipped through your fingers.

The clock strikes midnight, we sing *Auld Lang Syne* and make our New Year's Resolutions. 'I'm going to exercise more', 'I'm going to save more', or 'I'm going to quit smoking'. Are these goals? You start all enthusiastically for a couple of weeks and then life goes back to normal. Why? Your resolution wasn't a goal. It was the germ of one, but it missed a few key points. Goals have clarity and are actionable; you need to know what you want, and just as importantly, how you'll know when you have achieved it.

If you aren't a goal-setting person, just start small. What is something you want to achieve in the next 90 days? It can be anything. Once you have achieved one goal move on to the next one. Keep taking baby steps towards what you want, and you will get there.

The 'B' word

Budgets were designed for businesses to account for cash flow. However, they can be a good tool to help get you out of a financial hole, as the focus is on what comes in and goes out. But most of us fail at making them work.

I prefer a Money Plan. If you have goals you want to achieve, a Money Plan isn't that hard to implement as you know why you are making the changes and monitoring your spending. A Money Plan isn't about frugality or depriving yourself of the things you love, it's about making choices. 'If I choose this now, can I still achieve my goal by X time?'

A Money Plan isn't based on numbers alone, it's designed to ensure that you are meeting your needs which could be for time together (or apart) or eating healthy food. Aligning your Money Plan to your beliefs and your values helps keep you on track because you are doing what is right and best for you and your family.

Opposites attract

You and your partner may have completely different views about spending, saving, and debt. If you do, don't worry, these differences can become strengths rather than weaknesses. Understand what it's like to be in their shoes and how they see the world. By utilising open honest communication you can make it work.

If you are struggling to communicate about money (or anything else) and are beginning to wonder why you are in the relationship at all... go back to the start of the relationship and think about what it was that attracted you to each other in the first place. What was that moment when you fell in love and knew this was the person for you?

If you want to enhance your relationship, or are struggling a bit, a great resource is Gary Chapman's *5 Love Languages*.

What's Your Love Language?

While Dr Chapman's book, *The 5 Love Languages*, was originally written in 1992, it's still relevant today. The book came from years of notes Dr Chapman took when working with the couples he was counselling. He recognized a pattern. He realized that the couples were misunderstanding one another and each other's needs.

After reviewing all of his notes, he came up with the 5 Love Languages. These languages describe five ways that people receive and express love in a relationship. Knowing your partner's love language and letting them know yours can help you both feel loved and appreciated.

You can take the online quiz on the 5 Love Languages' website to find out what your love language is. I have summarized each of them here for you.

Words of Affirmation. Telling each other 'I love you'. Giving compliments, encouragement, leaving love notes, and frequent digital communication like texts. Written or spoken words of affection are really important to someone whose primary love language is words of affirmation. They make them feel appreciated and understood.

Acts of Service. It isn't just doing things for your partner. It's going out of your way to do them because you know that it makes them happy and makes their life easier. Things like making chicken soup when they are unwell. Running a bath for them at the end of a busy day. For this group, actions speak louder than words. It's about showing how much they are appreciated.

Quality Time. Uninterrupted time together–no phones, no children, no pets, no distractions. When you are together, listen actively, lots of eye contact, and be fully present in the moment with them. Undivided attention is what fills this person's love tank.

Gifts. Gift giving doesn't have to be expensive purchases, it might be a flower from the garden or something you have made. It's all about the process, thinking about the gift, choosing the object, and the emotion that goes along with it. For this group, giving meaningful things that matter and align with their values will light up their life and love.

Physical Touch. Holding hands, a hug first thing in the morning and last thing at night. Even just a hand on a shoulder will ensure this person feels loved. For them, physical touch is an incredible emotional connector.

Once you understand what each of your love languages are, you have another tool to apply to your communication toolbox. Bear in mind that relationships are complex and just applying love languages to your relationship isn't the be-all and end-all, but it's something you can easily implement into your relationship and see what happens.

What Have Love Languages Got To Do With Money?

Our love language can also influence how we spend our money. You can fulfil all the love languages without money, but some, like gifts, are often met by spending money and can sometimes get a bit out of hand.

This story came from a client. It was a special number birthday for her. Her husband (whose prime love language is gifts) commissioned a painting for her by one of her favourite local artists. She loves it! It was the perfect gift... but he didn't stop there. He also threw a very large party and invited the artist and his partner as guests of honour. The only problem was that the couple no longer lived locally, so it involved international flights and accommodation for the artist and his partner, plus a few touristy things, plus food, plus drink. Hubby got a huge shock when his wife threw her toys out of the cot at all the expense he had gone to and the money he had wasted. She just wanted a quiet dinner with him and time to gaze at the painting. Guess what her love language is? Quality time.

If you are a quality time person, you can fall into the trap of thinking that spending time together is always free, which it is if you choose to spend your quality time at home or going for walks. But it's very easy to get carried away in creating the atmosphere for quality time, like romantic dinners, going to shows, art gallery openings, and using money to pay for the quality time. Particularly if, like my client above, you are a Spender personality.

If you have a partner with time or acts of service love language, finding the time to do the little chores that make your partner feel loved can be a challenge. It's important to create the space in your busy day to make them breakfast, for example. A quality time person might go down the path of 'it's easier to pay someone else to do it'.

Physical touch is the easiest to keep consistently finance-free, but what if physical touch just isn't high on your radar? Maybe you know it is for your partner, so you could end up finding yourself sending them off to massages, facials, and pedicures to make sure they get their fill of physical touch in a 'safe' way.

Words of Affirmation is all about encouraging your partner about their ability to manage their money. This is particularly important if you have a Money Avoider personality who may be feeling a lack of confidence in this area.

There are a lot more variations and ways of fitting your Love Language and your Money Personality together; I have given you just a few to think about.

While it's lovely to have a surprise from your partner, you can talk about making sure you are meeting both your financial goals and your love languages in your Money Plan during your date night. I often find when working with couples that the most overlooked part of their finances is the relationship nurturing bucket. Particularly for parents, allowing the time and money to nurture their relationship tends to be pretty low on the priority list.

The key message here is when you look at your spending, think about your underlying love language as well as your money personality, as well as your beliefs and values.

Wow, that is a lot to think about. Is it any wonder this money stuff is so hard?

In Part Three, we are going to dive into the critical tools to help you apply what you have been learning.

LET'S PULL IT ALL TOGETHER
PART TWO - WRAP UP

Even among couples, money can be a taboo subject.

Part Two is about breaking the taboo and being able to talk about money in a loving peaceful way.

In Chapter 5 we looked at the differences between men and women when it comes to money that have come about from stereotypes and gender bias. Fortunately, they are changing, but you never know what is lurking in the background of your own money story, so it's time to get it out into the open.

There is no right or wrong about this, so don't judge yourself or your partner if you fit any of the stereotypes. All I want you to do is be aware that they exist, then as a couple, you can decide if they work for you or not.

Bear in mind that these are generalisations, and in your relationship, they may be the other way around, or you both share these feelings, or they may not apply to you at all.

What did you learn by looking at your family history?

Step back in time in Chapter 6 and look back into the early days of your relationship when you had the rose-tinted glasses on (as we all did).

Are the little habits that looked like fun through the rose-tinted view still that way now?

Talking about money is where this is all leading and we start to explore this in Chapter 7. First of all, establish where you fit on the spectrum of how you currently talk about money. Are you the silent type or the more vocal one? If you aren't ready to deep dive and have a money conversation yet, you can build up to it by learning more about your relationship with money. This might be a good place to go back to some of the exercises in Part One and review your answers and get some clarity about your journey before attempting to combine it with your partner.

We headed back to Money personalities in Chapter 8. You know what yours is, and you probably have a pretty good idea of what your partner's is, even if they haven't taken the quiz. If they haven't, I would encourage them to do so.

I hope you enjoyed the exercise of spending a day in each other's shoes. You will have come away with a real sense of what it's like to be opposites and how you can work with those differences.

Talking about how to debunk the myths and perceptions you have that come from your own view of the world as an Amasser and Money Monk can also lead to a greater understanding of each other's thoughts and values.

If you are living with an Avoider, then patience is the skill you need to practice.

Life is never perfect, except in the movies of course, so Chapter 9 is a reality check about the money arguments you are having. You might not be arguing about money, or you may be avoiding a money discussion, but whichever camp you are in, you need to know. All I want you to do is observe and write down your observations, thoughts, and feelings. Actions will follow in Part Three.

Financial Infidelity is a very difficult situation to address. The Relationship Index (in the bonus workbook www.moneymentalist.com/bookbonus) is a good starting point to establish if it is happening in your relationship and how serious it is.

You will see that the recurring theme in Chapters 7 through 10 is the money conversation. Effective communication about money is the foundation of a happy money marriage, which is what I talk about in Chapter 11. For some of you, this will be an aspirational goal, and for others, you will be much closer. Wherever you are on your journey, adding in your love language will enhance your conversations and understanding of what is important to each of you.

The Love Language quiz (also in your bonus workbook) is not only a great quiz for money, but it's also a nice way to remind yourself how you can show love to your partner through the love language that's important to them.

Once you understand how each other thinks, feels, and behaves with their money, you are all set to put some goals in place, build a Money Plan, and start to regularly connect about money when you have your financial date night.

The practical steps of how to do this are what you are moving on to in Part Three.

WHAT ELSE IS GOING ON? AND THE PRACTICAL APPLICATION

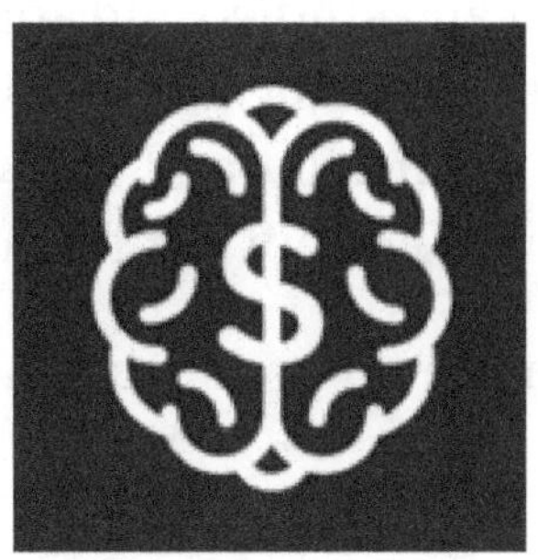

Wow, you've made it through two really incredibly powerful yet challenging sections of this book! Congratulations on coming this far. The things you've learnt so far are life-changing, on an individual level and relational level. I trust you're beginning to experience the effects of that already.

Understanding your relationship with money *and* how to merge that with someone else's are the keys that Gaz and I just didn't have. We thought the feelings we had for each other would be enough to ride out every storm. And we did, we rode out quite a few storms... but each storm left us further apart from one another because we were afraid of the difficult conversations.

Gaz didn't share with me how desperate he was feeling and how depression was closing in on him. He couldn't ask for help and

I didn't ask him to share the burden of our money worries. Gaz and I had the surprise gift of a final four weeks together; every hour was precious to us both. We learnt to forgive each other and ourselves. We learnt that love doesn't conquer all, *communication does*. I feel incredibly privileged that Gaz wanted me to be with him when he passed. He stayed as long as he could so we could say all we needed to say and heal all that needed to be healed. I know few people get this opportunity and I don't take it for granted.

It became clear to me in that hospice room why I do the work I do. Everything I learnt and studied and applied to my life pulled me back from the brink of financial ruin. It's the gift I needed to pull myself back up financially and show you how to do the same. It was too late for Gaz, but not for you and me.

No matter where you are on your journey, it's not too late for you.

Parts 1 and 2 of this book would be enough to send you off with and hope for the best. But knowledge alone doesn't change people, action does. That's why I'm including Part Three. This is where we get super actionable with practical steps and activities to get you moving forward, not just sitting and learning.

We will revisit some of the concepts from Parts 1 and 2 with a deep dive into steps you can take today, this week, and each day thereafter. Carve out some time to complete the exercises! I can't say this enough–I didn't write this book to fill your head with more information about money. And you didn't pick it up for kicks–you're looking for a change. The next pages hold the steps you need to achieve that change.

Consider Part Three where I take your hand and say, 'Let's do this together. Here's how'. If you do want to reach out and work with me one-to-one to do these steps with you, you can, just go to www.moneymentalist.com and book a time to meet with me.

Before you start diving into the exercises in the following chapters. I want to share a few other insights about your relationship with money.

This part of your relationship is below the surface, in your subconscious. You don't even know it's there until someone points it out. But it impacts your decisions about money all of the time. Marketers understand these concepts very well and utilize them to 'help' us make buying decisions. There is nothing wrong with this, they have a job to do. Once you understand these money fallacies and mental biases you will spot them and be able to make better decisions.

The first thing you need to realise is that we are human. This means we are not rational, we make decisions based on emotion. Our emotions kick in about 10 seconds before our rational brain engages and slow us down long enough to think about the decision we are about to make. You can spend a lot of money in 10 seconds. Time yourself the next time you pull out the credit card or click 'add to cart' when you are in the mood to buy something.

The number one rule I have for myself is the 10-second rule. Bear in mind that my money personality is Amasser/Spender so I am more likely to spend impulsively than a Hoarder personality will. If I'm out and I see something I'd like to buy, I make myself walk on by (I think that's a song), do the rest of my errands, and return to decide if I really want the item. I may or may not purchase it. Sometimes I don't bother going back at all. I give my rational brain time to kick in and go through my mental checklist and think about why I want to buy. I also consider whether I have the money right now, if it will serve a purpose in my life, bring me joy, or fulfil a need. By the time I have done all of this I know I am making a good decision. For larger purchases, I give myself at least 24 hours. That gives me time to get through the rationalization and justification phase as well.

The number two rule I have for myself is that I don't save my credit card number on any of the online shopping sites I use. This means I have to move, find my purse, pull out the credit card, and refresh the site. This takes me more than 10 seconds and gives me time to go through my checklist above. Quite often I become one of those annoying shoppers who click out before completing the purchase.

A little aside here, for my Hoarder readers who are paired with a Spender: I have just given you insight into how our minds work. You can help distract your Spender partner with the mental checklist in a loving, caring way, not judgmental or critical. You have your own way of doing things that your Spender partner also needs to understand.

Since the 1980s there has been growth in the area of Behavioural Economics. I think of Behavourial Economics like this: it combines traditional economic theory (which assumes we are rational) with psychology (which knows that we aren't). Combining the two helps us understand why we behave the way we do in reality, not the way theory thinks we should. It is a fascinating and enlightening area of research. In the next chapter, I am going to give you a little taste of behavioural economics and how it relates to your money behaviour.

Let's go!

CHAPTER 12

WHY WE DO DUMB STUFF WITH OUR MONEY

Have you ever done something and then afterwards scratched your head and thought, *What on earth was I thinking!?* Welcome to the world of being human. We are not rational and despite our best intentions, there are going to be times when we do odd things.

So, what influences our decisions? There is a wealth of research into why we do dumb stuff–technically called Behavioural Economics. As Dan Ariely, Professor of Psychology and Behavioral Economics at Duke University, says, 'We're predictably irrational!'

We are going to spend a little bit of time exploring some of the reasons why we do dumb stuff with our money. The good news is that once you are aware of these money biases you can easily monitor yourself and break them.

Instant Gratification – I want it all and I want it now!

I know we have all had that Freddie Mercury moment. 'I want it all and I want it now.' That is what instant gratification is all about.

Like me, you've probably heard your parents and grandparents talk about when they were young and had to save up to buy what

133

they wanted, and your eyes roll back in your head because *it's just not like that anymore, Granny.*

We can have whatever we want whenever we want it. They ask, 'How can you do that?' It's called credit, Granny!

It isn't just that little piece of plastic, it's also all the other buy-now, pay-later types of deals that enable us to satisfy our wants and needs *right now.*

What does credit do? It separates the pain of having to pay from the pleasure of getting it now. Here's an example: I like to flex my instant gratification muscle every once in a while and give myself a test. I draw out a $50 note from my bank account and pop it into my wallet. The test is to see how long I can keep that $50 intact. How long can I delay gratification and not spend that cash? My current $50 note has been in my wallet now for two months. This doesn't mean I haven't spent money, I have used my debit and credit card numerous times, but something holds me back from handing over my cash. That is, until I'm in a situation, usually a farmer's market, where the stall owner doesn't have an electronic option. I look longingly at what I want to buy, think about it long and hard, and then happily hand over my $50 note. I get my purchase and some change. This is the pain-pleasure principle in action. I've gone through the pain of paying and the pleasure of receiving something that I want in return. But once I have the change and my lovely $50 note is no longer intact, the rest of the cash can disappear very quickly. Without the same level of consideration and thought, it just slips through my fingers, it's $10 here, $3.00 there, small insignificant amounts on small insignificant things.

But when it comes to credit, our brain doesn't quite see it like that. All it sees is pleasure, pleasure, pleasure, pleasure. I've got all of this stuff, but I haven't had to pay for it yet. That's what we mean by instant gratification.

Unless you actually look at your credit card statement, you can defer the pain indefinitely... at least until the card stops working!

Start practising delayed gratification rather than instant gratification. In the long term, it's much better for you. Have a savings account for the fun things you want. Train your brain that saving is as much fun as spending. The way to do this is to open a bank account, give it a really fun nickname, and reward yourself for good behaviour. When you say no to something, from the muffin with your coffee to the second item because it's 50% off, transfer the amount of money you *would have* spent into your good behaviour account. At the end of the month have a look at the balance and see what you would like to do with the money–save some, spend some, donate some, or roll it over into the next month.

A few years ago, Simon and I were planning a trip to Vietnam with our friends. I decided to call my good behaviour account "Steps to Vietnam". I worked out a formula and based on the number of steps I walked each day, I transferred a few dollars to my "Steps to Vietnam" account each week. I had a year to save for the trip, and I reached both my savings and my fitness goal in nine months!

There is a very famous study on delayed gratification often called the Marshmallow Test. In the late 1960s/early 1970s, Professor Walter Mischel (Stanford University) studied a group of 4- to 6-year-olds, who were left in a room for 15 minutes with a marshmallow. They were given the option of eating the marshmallow now or getting two if they waited 15 minutes. Some were able to wait, they displayed delayed gratification, and others couldn't, they scarfed the marshmallow and didn't get the second one. This group wanted instant gratification.

You can watch clips on YouTube that show the lengths some children will go to not eat the marshmallow! The study has since been replicated many times, which you can find online as well. For a bit of fun, in the workbook (http://www.money mentalist.com/bookbonus) I have included the link to one of my favourite clips.

What makes this study interesting is that the researchers continue to follow these children, now adults. They have found that 40 years later those who could delay gratification have better social skills, and are less likely to be obese or abuse substances. They are more self-motivated, dependable, and generally score better in other life measures as well.

This leads to the question: are you born with the ability to delay gratification, or can you learn it?

Let's go back to the marshmallow test and look at the twist the researchers from the University of Rochester added.

They split the children into two groups before offering them the marshmallow. The first group was exposed to an 'unreliable experience'. The child had a box of crayons and the researcher promised to bring a larger box but never did. In the second group the children were exposed to a 'reliable experience', the promised crayons arrived.

When it came to the marshmallow test, those in the first group had no reason to trust the researcher, so most ate the marshmallow in a fairly short space of time, whilst those in the second group had learned two things:

- Waiting is worth it.
- I can wait.
- I can trust they will deliver on the promise of a second marshmallow.

On average, the second group waited to eat the marshmallow four times longer than the first group. What the researchers concluded is that the ability to delay gratification isn't a predetermined trait but is impacted by experience and environment and therefore can be learned. Which is good news for anyone over six years old!

You can train yourself to delay gratification by starting small–promise something to yourself and then deliver it. Keep doing this over and over–your brain will rewire and say, 'Yes, waiting is worth it, and I *can* wait!'. Delaying gratification is better.

Here are five strategies for delaying gratification:

1. Know your values. We covered this in Part One.

2. Know where you want to go. Have clear goals.

3. Have a plan. Use a roadmap to get you where you want to go.

4. Set your priorities. Which is more important right now, *this* or *that*?

5. Reward yourself. If your goal is a long way out, then break it down into smaller chunks so you can reward yourself for delaying gratification along the way.

A young couple I worked with did this well. They were saving hard for the deposit on their first home. They added in a little extra savings each month. When they reached a pre-determined target in their savings account, they bought something they wanted for their new home, but they wouldn't use the items until they had the home. It was something small, like some glassware or new linen. These items gave them pleasure and anticipation which motivated them to reach the goal of buying their own home so they could use these items.

This is reminiscent of when I was a teenager and had a 'glory box'. I accumulated household things that I would use when I left home. Thinking about this now, I realise I'm still using some of the crockery I bought way back then!

Keeping Up With The Joneses

Conspicuous spending, keeping up with the 'Joneses', or using money as a status symbol used to be thought of as limited to the rich and famous. Well, not anymore. We can all keep up with the Joneses because of credit!

Why do we feel the need to keep up with the Joneses? I see this frequently with clients. 'We couldn't possibly cancel the holiday; the Joneses took their holiday and how will it look if we cancel ours?' So what? What is more important, looking good or staying afloat financially? Well, it seems for many people it's looking good.

I read the novel, *The Deaths,* by Mark Lawson. There are several really great one-liners and this one is my favourite:

'We were keeping up with the Joneses, but the Joneses were broke!'

This is what happens when you start keeping up with the Joneses–you have no idea who the *Joneses* are trying to keep up with or if they're faking their ability to afford their lifestyle too!

Keeping up with the Joneses isn't exclusive to the supposed 'rich', it's prevalent everywhere, from the teenager who has to have the latest designer clothes and phone to look 'cool' to the business owner driving around in the latest car while their taxes go unpaid. It also applies to non-financial areas of life, like the stay-at-home mum who has to lose her baby fat six weeks after birth to look 'normal' on Instagram!

Why do we do this to ourselves? A lot of it has to do with peer pressure from friends, workmates, and what we see in the media, as well as the desire to have the newest and best.

Plus, we love to show off; we want to be seen as successful. Splashing the cash around does just this.

The easy availability of credit enables us to do this. We no longer work hard and save for what we want; instant gratification is rife. It gives us the illusion of being cool and successful.

It also comes from within us and our level of self-esteem. We think we need to look and behave a certain way and have the right 'toys' to impress others to make ourselves feel happy.

But success shouldn't be about money! There are other important factors of success, like family, happiness, and feeling good about ourselves.

How do we stop keeping up with the Joneses?

Understand the difference between *your* needs and wants and those of others. What is important to you and your family?

Have clear goals that give you focus and something to work towards. When you get the urge to keep up with the Joneses, you can ask the question: 'Do I really need the new (insert your own word here), or do I just want it to look cool on socials?'

Decide what 'enough' is—how much stuff do you really need to make you happy?

Once you make yourself and your goals the number one priority, you will be surprised to see how much easier it is to say no and not worry so much about what everyone else thinks.

I worked with a client who came to me because she was close to retirement and still had a mortgage; it was weighing her down.

When we first started to talk, it seemed obvious to me that she needed to downsize and move to a different area, as this would give her some capital. No mortgage and no stress! But it wasn't that easy. Where she lived was the 'right' address and where she wanted to downsize was also the 'right address', but she simply couldn't afford to live in either 'right address'. I asked her to write down what she wanted in a home, the environment she'd like, what was important to her now, and where she wanted to be in five years. Once she reflected on this, she realized it wasn't the address that was important, her priorities were the environment and getting rid of stress. She looked a couple of suburbs away to an 'okay' address and found the perfect home for her. Five years later she is loving life, has no debt, and has no regrets about the move. And of course, over time her 'okay' address has become a more desirable area as well.

Anchoring

At some time or other, we have all been anchored. Anchoring is everywhere, not just in the world of money.

What is anchoring? It's a term used in Behavioural Economics to describe an irrational bias we have to a benchmark figure. What does that mean in English? We latch onto 'something', and we base our decision-making around that 'something'. That 'something' may have nothing to do with the decision we are trying to make, and often we don't even know the anchor is there. The initial anchor (whether it's right or wrong), becomes our reference point for our future decision-making.

There are several ways anchoring impacts our decisions, from how we decide the value of our house to how we decide how much a pair of socks should be.

When we want to purchase something, anchoring tends to happen more often when we are purchasing a product or service that we don't know too much about. Here's how it works.

I was happily driving my car when it developed a bit of a shudder through the steering wheel. I didn't think it was major so I took it to my local tyre shop, thinking my wheels just needed balancing. (That is about the extent of my technical knowledge of tyres). I left my car in the serviceman's capable hands and headed off to my appointment.

Within 10 minutes my phone rang–never a good sign. It was the tyre shop. The problem was somewhat more serious than balancing. I needed a new tyre as this one was falling apart (apparently I was lucky I made it to the tyre shop without having a serious accident). Not only did I need one new tyre, but the others were also looking quite worn, so I really needed to replace all four. This was not what I wanted to hear, but safety comes first, so I took a deep breath and asked for the price.

This is what I was told.

'We can get you XYZ brand which is a top-of-the-line tyre for your car and they are $279 each.

Or, we can get you ABC brand which is also a good brand and they are $220 each, and then, of course, there are the under $200 imported ones but we really wouldn't recommend those.'

Here was my dilemma. I didn't know the difference between XYZ and ABC brands. After asking a couple more questions, I was told that the ABC brand was comparable with what I had on the car and was reliable, so I chose that option and felt quite happy with my decision as I had 'saved' $59 per tyre.

What had happened here? The anchoring effect had kicked in.

I didn't know a lot about what I was purchasing so when I was told \$279.00 for a 'top-of-the-line tyre' I subconsciously attached my decision-making to that number.

I was given a second option that was almost as good but at a lower price, so I selected *that* option as it sounded like a really good deal.

The anchoring effect is something to use to your advantage when you are the seller.

I told this story to our friend who is an insurance broker. He uses this tactic all the time when talking to clients. He gives them three options: one with all the bells and whistles with a high premium, a second option almost as good at a lower premium, and the third covers the bare minimum. The most common choice is the mid-price option. He knew the system worked but hadn't realised why.

As a buyer, be aware of anchoring and wherever possible make sure you do your research before committing so you set your own anchor.

Behavioural Economics has lots of examples of the anchoring effect and how it works. It's fascinating how our brains attach to information that in some cases has no relevance to our decisions. If you want to learn more about this, Dan Ariely has a whole chapter on it in his book *Predictably Irrational*.

Once we have been anchored and made our decision, the next bias kicks in...

Confirmation Bias and Decision-Making

I love my new tyres! They were a real bargain and the brand has the best reliability and durability in the market. That is my story and I'm sticking to it, and you can't tell me anything different because I won't believe you! Welcome to the world of confirmation bias.

What is confirmation bias all about? Why do we need to be aware of it?

In a nutshell, confirmation bias is the way we pick data to confirm our beliefs. We look for information that confirms our views and ratifies our decisions. This happens both consciously and unconsciously.

Not only do we look for information that confirms our beliefs, but we also actively discount and don't listen to information that is contrary to our belief about a product, person, investment strategy, and so on.

Confirmation bias is everywhere. It doesn't impact only decisions about money, but also our impressions of people.

A few years ago, one of my girlfriends started dating a new man. His introduction to the group (there were eight of us) didn't go well, and we unanimously agreed that he was unsuitable for her and a bit of an idiot. We didn't tell her that of course. But confirmation bias had kicked in and over the next couple of years, as far as we were concerned, our first impression was constantly reinforced, despite our girlfriend telling us how wonderful he was; we continually found fault and overlooked any positives. I should add that they are now happily married. Do the rest of us still think he's an idiot? Well, that's for us to know.

Confirmation bias can also work the other way around, where you constantly see positives and overlook the red flags. You may have employed someone to work in your business who, on paper, looked like an ideal candidate. But after a short period, the cracks started to show and others had to do their work because the person you employed was incompetent. You won't see this because you're busy being impressed that they turn up on time and stay late and are so good with the clients. Yes, I have been guilty of this in the past, as have many other employers who find themselves losing top staff members and wondering how it happened.

So confirmation bias is part of our everyday life, not just our relationship with money.

Let's talk briefly about our friendly marketers and brands and how confirmation bias can work in their favour. This could be any product from cereal to clothes to cars to investment funds. In every sector, the marketer's plan is the same.

'Let's spend lots of money on advertising and get the product anchored in our customer's head. We will tell them how wonderful our product is, they'll buy it, and once they are our customer, they won't listen to our opposition and will be our loyal customer.' For a while, anyway.

Think how much brand loyalty costs you. I shudder to think how much my loyalty to a particular skincare range has cost me over the years! Not only that, I introduced my daughter to it at a young age and now she is hooked as well.

So, how do you overcome confirmation bias? Becoming aware of what a confirmation bias is and how it can affect our thinking is a good starting point but here are three practical suggestions:

1. Start monitoring your choices. Look back at some of your past purchases; for example, do you see a pattern of brand loyalty for no logical reason? 'Just because you always have', isn't a reason to continue to do the same. This is illustrated well in the TV show *Eat Well for Less*. The show's hosts swap out various items of food for

different brands, often at a lower cost. They plain-package everything and see if the family accepts the change and can tell the difference between their usual brand and the replacement.

2. Start asking yourself questions. Is this assumption correct? Am I getting both sides of the story and, more to the point, am I taking both into account? Be your own 'devil's advocate'.

3. Check your reasoning. You might want to check with a friend or colleague for a second opinion before purchasing a big-ticket item. Be open to listening to their feedback. Make sure you don't ask someone who is simply going to say what you want to hear.

We Rationalise And Justify Our Spending

I bet you didn't know you are an author, did you? Whether you recognise it or not, we all tell ourselves stories to justify and rationalise our spending. Some of those stories are short blogs and others are full-length novels! Some of these stories are in our heads and others we share with our loved ones and friends.

What do I mean by justifying and rationalising our spending? I looked in the Merriam-Webster dictionary to see what it had to say about 'justify'. It says, 'To provide good reason for the actions of [someone]'.

Interesting. What about rationalise? 'To think about or describe something (such as bad behaviour) in a way that explains it and makes it seem proper, more attractive, etc.'.

Those two definitions sum it up. Here's an example.

I was at a dinner party recently and the usual question of 'What do you do?' came up. Generally, one of two things happens when I say I am a Money Mentor. The person suddenly has to go and talk to someone else (the same thing happened when I used to say I was an accountant). Or I get chapter and verse about how good (or bad) they are with money.

This particular evening, I ended up in quite an animated conversation with a couple I didn't know particularly well. Every second sentence was a justification or rationalisation for their decisions. Here is a snippet towards the end of the conversation.

'We spend everything we earn, but that's okay because we have investments which will generate income when we retire.'

'What type of investments?' I politely asked.

'Commercial property. We have great tenants and they cover all the costs, so it doesn't cost us a penny. We do have a big mortgage, but it's tax-deductible.'

I couldn't resist; I had to ask how long until they retire.

'Two years', they replied. At that point, I bit my tongue and decided I needed to circulate the room again.

Let's just unpack this conversation.

1. This couple is two years away from retirement and the end of their big salary, so their income will be dropping.

2. They currently spend all of their income so they aren't adding to their retirement fund, reducing debt or anything else to prepare for the loss of earnings.

3. They have an investment property that has debt on it that is going to take longer than two years to pay off. They are totally reliant on their tenant to do this for them.

From where I was sitting, this just didn't make sense to me as a Money Mentor or accountant.

Over the years they have rationalised and justified their standard of living and spending habits on the premise that they will be secure in retirement because they have an investment property with the bonus of tax deductibility.

This is pretty high on the scale of justifying behaviour.

I'm sure we've all been in a situation (I know I have) where you want to buy something that we know we shouldn't. We do the maths to break it down into a daily cost and decide we can afford it; we will just cut back somewhere else.

The long-term impact of this type of rationalising isn't quite the same as the couple above who were gambling with their retirement.

We rationalise and justify our spending to make ourselves feel better about our actions. The scary thing is that we aren't consciously aware that this is what we are doing. We probably don't want to know because then we'd have to face making decisions that may not be as good as we thought. And we probably should have said no!

David Krueger, in his book *The Secret Language of Money*, puts it like this: 'The goal of cost justification is nearly always the same; legitimising an expense that we know is of questionable legitimacy' and, 'Rationalisation is the articulation of seemingly good reasons for bad decisions'.

How do you cure yourself of these types of thoughts and behaviours patterns? The only way to do it is to put yourself under the spotlight. For some decisions, it's best to do this with an independent person. Examine the decision in terms of the big picture and not just in isolation.

Ask yourself questions like:

- How does this fit in with the plan I have for my future (eg. the goals that you set in Part Two)?

- Am I spending this to feel good? (Think about your money personality as well.)

- Am I buying this because I deserve it? Watch how many times you use this argument, particularly on lower-cost decisions, where justification is easier.

- What impact is this decision going to have in one year? Five years? Ten years?

My challenge to you is to have a look at your most recent purchase and examine the stories you told yourself at the time. If you are honest with yourself, was it a good decision or not?

Internal Bargaining

I'll have one more cookie, then I will stop; I'll start my diet tomorrow. This is your thought process as you reach into the cookie jar again, even though you know you should have stopped at one and not eaten the whole jar!

'I'll just buy this and then nothing more until next month.' We say this to ourselves as we purchase yet another article of clothing, gizmo, or toy for our children.

These are both examples of internal bargaining. You have set a future commitment, to start your diet or not to spend, so you feel quite virtuous and can justify your excess. I have a number of clients who do a big spend before contacting me, just in case I tell them they have to stop spending (which isn't how I work, but they don't know that coming in!).

Internal bargaining doesn't help you lose weight, nor does it help you manage your spending.

Once you know you have a habit of doing this type of bargaining with yourself, you can pull yourself up and put the brakes on.

Sunk Costs

Sometimes we start with a purchase that may have been budgeted for, thought out, and good! But when the purchase takes a turn, like a house renovation that becomes a never-ending money pit, we can find it hard to abandon the plan, even if doing so would save us the loss of more funds. This is also known as the Sunk Cost Fallacy, yet another form of overspending that we can slip into without realising. We may know we are taking on extra debt or taking from our ability to purchase other things we need, knowing we might have to wait a long time to recover the costs, if at all.

Sunk Costs are everywhere and they don't occur only in your finances or business. Have you sat through a really bad movie thinking, *Oh well, I've watched an hour so I may as well watch the rest.* Gottcha! You have just succumbed to a sunk cost.

'In for a penny, in for a pound', my dad would say as we headed to the local eat-all-you-want buffet restaurant for a family dinner. 'I've paid my $25 (okay, this was a little while ago), so I'm going to get my money's worth and eat as much as I can'. Over the course of the next couple of hours, he was true to his word and had eaten for the sake of eating, 'getting his money's worth' almost to the point of bursting!

We keep making decisions (monetary or otherwise) based on how much we've already spent on a project. It's hard to let go of something that is going backwards or to not complete an expensive project even though the cost of continuing just isn't logical.

'You have to put a stop to this, this business just isn't going to work. You're just throwing good money after bad and it's jeopardising your other businesses'. This was a conversation I was having with one of my clients.

In my view it was clear that the business was losing a lot of money and throwing more money at it wasn't going to help. The rational decision was to stop, sell what we could to recover some of the investment, and move on to the next project.

But from the owner's perspective, he had sunk a significant amount of money and time into this venture and wasn't prepared to cut his losses and walk away just yet. Emotions had overridden his business sense and admitting that he had made the wrong decision and lost money just wasn't an option.

We get caught up in the Sunk Cost Fallacy because we emotionally invest in the resources, money or time that we have committed in the past and that impacts how we assess what we are going to do in the future.

Here are some tips to help you recognise and avoid these sunk costs:

1. Before you start a major project, do some serious planning. Define what you want to achieve and how much time, effort, energy, and money you are prepared to commit to the project.

2. Set some targets and accountabilities along the way, in other words, monitor the project to make sure it's on track and on budget. If it isn't, pause, re-evaluate, and decide at that point about how to proceed.

3. Have someone else look over your shoulder. It's easier for another person to identify sunk costs than it is for you to see through the cloud of emotion, i.e. you can't see the trees for the forest!

4. Be prepared to walk away. You have spent the time, money, and resources and now they are gone, never to return. Get over it and move on.

5. Write a pros and cons list. If the only pro on the list is you feeling better emotionally about the project, then stop!

The Framing Effect

Depending on how something is presented to us, it can change our decision-making process. This is something that marketers are very good at doing when pricing goods and also during that favourite time of mine... the sales and discounts!

Let me take you to the supermarket. You are in the meat department and there are two packs of steak; you are trying to choose which one to have. They both weigh the same but one is labelled '75% lean' and the other is labelled '25% fat'.

Which one would you choose?

In a study focused on the Framing Effect, most people chose 75% lean; it sounds healthier and more positive than 25% fat. But both packs are the same.

What if the 75% lean was more expensive than the 25% fat, would you still buy it? Quite possibly, particularly if you are prepared to pay more for 'healthy' food.

When I'm racing around the supermarket, I don't study every label and price in detail. You probably won't notice the framing either–that both packs are the same yet at a different price.

Another way that framing can catch us is by thinking in terms of percentages rather than dollars.

I have done this myself without realising it. I have driven to a shopping centre 40 kilometres out of my way to save 25% on a $20 set of mixing bowls and patted myself on the back for a great deal.

But I couldn't be bothered to drive into the city (20 kilometres away) to pay $190 for a dress when my local shop had the same thing for $200–it wasn't worth the effort to save 'only' $10.

Let's do the maths for both of these purchases. The 25% discount on my mixing bowls saved me $5.00. I probably spent about that in fuel costs driving 40km, not to mention the extra time it took me to drive there.

The $10 savings on my dress wasn't worth my time and effort of driving 20km. If we reframe that to a percentage, it was only a 5% savings, so in this case, it was probably a good decision based on the travel time and fuel costs, plus how I value my time.

My logic doesn't look quite so logical on my mixing bowls. I went to all that time and extra expense to 'save' $5.00–the way the deal was framed, it sounded too good to turn down. I should have done the maths before I left home! I saved $5 but probably spent the same to save it.

The moral of the story is to take a bit more time when you think something looks like a good deal; it's framed by marketers to make you think that way.

Do the maths when you are looking at percent savings, convert it to dollars, and see if it's worth your time and effort to go the extra distance or not.

Our next bias Mental Accounting is closely related to Framing.

Mental Accounting

You didn't know you were an accountant, did you? No, mental accounting doesn't mean sitting there with your calculator and adding up receipts. Mental accounting was identified by Richard Thaler, a behavioural economist. Whether we know it or want to, we naturally organise, evaluate, and keep track of our finances.

We all have little buckets in our heads and we assign different types of money to different buckets and we treat them differently. You might have a rent bucket, you might have a holiday bucket, and you might have a Friday night spending bucket.

What happens if you want to go out on a Friday night and your Friday night bucket is empty? You might be tempted to 'borrow' from another bucket. You may be reluctant to borrow from your 'savings for an overseas holiday bucket'. You view the meaning of that bucket and its contents differently. It's serious saving money versus fun money. That's what the concept of mental accounting is all about, and you do it all the time even if you aren't aware of it. If you are struggling with pinching money from your bucket, then think about it like this: if this bucket I'm about to 'pinch' from was my salary, (which is our 'serious' money buckets as it has to pay for all of our living costs first), would I still spend this money this way? In other words, is there enough left over after I have paid for food, power, rent, phone etc for me to go out on Friday night? If your mental accounting answer if no, then you'll probably stay home and invite your friend over to watch a movie.

Why is this important? We think of money differently when we've assigned it for a particular purpose.

Here's another example. I encourage business owners to have a savings account called Tax. The savings that go into that account now has a label, and mental accounting takes over. The money in this account is earmarked for a specific purpose and doesn't get withdrawn for any other purpose. This is a great way to save for other things as well, like an overseas holiday, a new car, etc. The more our mind relates to what the money is for, the more likely we are to only use it for that purpose. When you are setting up bank accounts to save for a specific purpose, give the account a nickname that relates to that purpose and excites you.

You can also create physical barriers by having a coin jar (for those who still carry cash) and labelling the jar for a specific purpose. That way you don't tend to dip into it when you run out of milk or fancy a coffee as you are heading out the door. This is great for children's pocket money as well. You may even label that jar 'fun money' so you *can* grab that coffee or milk if the money jar can afford it!

There can also be a downside to mental accounting.

Think about the times you opened a birthday card from your grandparents and found a $20 note in there. Did you save it? Probably not. You more than likely spent it on something for yourself. That's okay if you are a child and you don't have bills to pay. We attach sentimentality to our mental accounting that says, 'Grandma would have wanted me to enjoy this money; so I won't pay off my credit card debt (or tuck it away in my retirement savings), I will have a spontaneous unplanned overseas trip instead'. I'm not saying this is a bad thing. I just want you to be aware of how mental accounting works so that you can take a bit of time to decide what to do with Grandma's inheritance and not look back in a few years with regret.

You may be looking forward to your quarterly bonus. Be wary of mental accounting here as well. It goes something like this. 'Well, I never had the money, so I won't miss it, so let's just spend it'. By the way, this can also happen when you receive an inheritance, a tax refund, or win the lottery.

Here are a few tips to help you get your mental accounting calculator working for you:

1. Do nothing for a few days. Simply let your windfall sit in your bank account and let the excitement die down.

2. Make a list of all the possible ways you can use the money. Be practical as well as fanciful. Include the mortgage and the dentist bill coming up in a couple of months. Add in the weekend away with friends or the watch you've been drooling over.

3. Now get out the calculator. Let your logical and rational brain take over. Prioritise the list and with your partner (or a close friend) decide how you want to allocate the bonus. There are no hard and fast rules here, you just want someone to challenge you on the decisions you're making to ensure you don't end up regretting them in a couple of months.

4. Wait a few more days, check the list, make some changes, and then take action. That may mean you leave the money in the bank; remember you don't have to spend it all.

Here are a couple more biases from the world of Behavioural Economics:

Loss Aversion

We don't like to lose money. You hear the term loss aversion a lot in the investment world when shares are going down. People sell because they're scared rather than hanging on and waiting for stocks to rise. If you are an investor then you need to understand loss aversion and how it impacts you personally in terms of your risk profile. Your authorized financial adviser can help you with your portfolio, including how to structure it.

Loss aversion is not only about investments, we also see it in other areas as well. For example, let's say you have $300,000 of net assets (this is the difference between everything you own, less how much money you owe) and you sell your car and lose $500. You really feel that loss of $500. It's a very tiny, tiny portion of your net assets, but you only relate it to that number. 'I've lost $500.' We do the same thing with a gain; we have gained $500.

Loss aversion affects different people in different ways. For example, loss aversion for the elderly can be very serious because they may not have the time to wait for the upswing to recover the loss. The advice they receive from their financial advisor is crucial to supporting them through the dips. If you have parents or grandparents, be aware that losing money is a huge fear for them, so be very gentle. They probably don't need to hear about the latest Bitcoin decline or the doom and gloom in the marketplace, as it could unsettle them even more.

We also feel a loss twice as much as we do a gain. This means if you lose $100, you need to gain $200 to feel as if you are in the same place.

Endowment Effect

The Endowment Effect is a by-product of Loss Aversion. We think everything that we own is worth more than market value because we own it. We have an emotional and symbolic attachment to it so we place a higher value on it than we would place on the same item if somebody else owned it.

What? How does this work? Here's an example. You and I have the same car. It's the same make and model, the same year, and very close in mileage. My car, of course, has been very well looked after over the years, so it must be worth more than yours. You, on the other hand, are thinking the same thing—your car has also been very well looked after so must be worth more than mine! You can see how this can make striking a deal difficult and where the art of negotiation comes into play. We can obviously sort this out otherwise we'd never buy or sell anything. But it does make it difficult for us to assign real market value because we always think that our stuff is better than your stuff when it comes to price.

There are times when we dig our toes in and refuse to part with the thing, holding out for a better price that we just *know* is out there, only to find out months later that the market price decreased and we end up selling for less anyway. I have done this myself when selling a piece of jewellery. I turned down a very motivated purchaser who didn't reach the price I wanted. I ended up selling it a few months later for a few hundred dollars less than the original offer.

The Endowment Effect is also something our friendly marketers love to use as well. They will try to inspire us and build a sense of connection to and ownership of the product so that we will happily pay more. Now that you know about the Endowment Effect you will be able to recognize when you are being manipulated and take a step back from the purchase.

Extrapolation Error

We are great predictors of the future based on the past. We are wired to do this. Our brain anticipates the repetition after it has happened twice before. It goes like this, 'My house has gone up 10% in value for the last two years, so it will do the same again this year' and we make a decision for the future based on the past. It's one of the main reasons we repeat financial mistakes. It is also a very common error for investors.

Research will help with this error. Recognize that you are automatically going to predict the outcome, so research back more than two years. Look at the best-case/worst-case scenario and decide if you can live with the worst-case option.

Invincibility Bias

This is closely related to the Extrapolation Error. We all know that bad stuff can happen, but we assume it won't happen to us. It looks like this: Your business is going from strength to strength, you've had two amazing years of growth, so you know the next one is going to be great too (extrapolation error). Then a competitor arrives in town—you're not worried, your business will be fine. Competitors come and go, but it won't affect me (invincibility bias). But it does and your business starts to decline.

As with many of these biases, once you know they exist, you can plan and make sure that you are taking the steps to protect your livelihood, your home, and your family.

This is just a taster of some of the Money Biases that affect the way we behave with our money. If you want to learn more, check out Dan Ariely and the other well-known experts in this area.

THE PRACTICAL SIDE OF A HAPPY MONEY MARRIAGE

You are now ready to dive into the longer and more detailed exercises. As you work through these exercises, make sure you have your journal handy as your off-the-top-of-your-head answers will be the starting point for these exercises. These are designed to be a bit repetitive to help you dig a little deeper each time. So, get comfy, turn off any distractions, put the kids to bed, shut the cat outside, get some water and snacks, and of course for some of the exercises, your partner. Settle in to work on the practical aspects of how to keep the money side of your relationship harmonious. You will not get through all of these exercises in one go. I recommend that you don't even try. You will get overwhelmed. Set aside no more than one hour or so at a time and gently ease yourself in. Take a break if you need to—you don't know what emotions will come up for you as you work through the exercises.

I know when I did the individual exercises, I experienced all of the emotions, from shame, to anger, to grief, to happiness. It is a lot to take in so be kind to yourself.

The first three exercises are for you to work on individually. They build on the questions I asked you in Part One. You don't have to do these exercises before you have the joint conversations. You may find that you start the money conversation for couples and then come back to the individual ones. It's entirely up to you. You know yourself and your partner, there is no right or wrong way to do this. Go with what feels right for you. If you prefer to, you can download the bonus workbook and exclusive readers free gifts here www.moneymentalist.com/bookbonus.

#1: Conversation with Money Exercise

To help understand your view of money better, pretend you are having a conversation with money.

Imagine what it looks like and what it might say to you if it got the chance.

Write down your dialogue–back and forth with questions and comments.

Here is an example: Sharon moved to a new city and misses her friends so she's spending lots of money going to bars to stop feeling lonely. Her salary isn't enough to cover the additional spending so she pays only the minimum balance on her credit card. She doesn't want to ask her parents for help.

She is lonely and has a money problem and they are feeding each other.

Sharon imagined money as a fun-loving companion, just like her, dressed in gothic-style black to attract attention.

This is how her money conversation went:

Sharon: I wish you'd hang around more often. It seems like every chance we have to get together you leave me.

Money: Well, ditto, I enjoy your company as well. But truthfully, I'm not sure you want to hear what I have to say.

Sharon: Go on, I can handle it. I want to know how you feel. I mean, c'mon, look at the things we've done together.

Money: See, that's just what I mean. I don't think you take our relationship seriously. You look to me for fun and entertainment, like that is all I can provide. It makes me feel cheap and used. I have so many more qualities that you don't seem to have noticed. I guess you make me feel worthless.

Sharon: Really? I thought you enjoyed the things we've done. Fun times make you feel worthless? Fun times are made possible because of you. I'm shocked, Money. I didn't sense that you were struggling with anything.

Money: That's just the point. You didn't sense it.

Sharon: What do you mean?

Money: You are so involved with *your* good time that you neglect the larger picture. You're so focused on the present, you don't see that maybe I have more to offer than just being a social support system. I do enjoy that, don't get me wrong, but even chocolate loses its appeal if that's all you eat.

Sharon: I see. I had no idea you felt this cheap.

Money: I don't think I'm the one you should be apologising to.

Sharon: What? You just told me my actions make you feel cheap.

Money: I'm not worried about my well-being. I am, however, concerned about the well-being of our relationship. I don't get what sort of life you're living.

Sharon: Yeah, but I don't know what I can do about it.

Money: You can change. I'm sure you have more that interests you than those hoppin' bars.

Sharon: I guess so, but I panic without other people.

Money: Why don't you challenge yourself?

Sharon: Money, you are tough. But you're right. Too much chocolate... Okay, I get it.

(extract from the book Crazy about Money. Maggie Baker, PhD.)

Olivia Mellan, in her book *Money Harmony,* recommends five steps for writing your conversation with money which also includes an internal commentary:

1. Have a conversation with money about how the relationship is going. The length of the conversation is up to you. Just go at your own pace and continue until you feel it winding down. Let yourself be surprised by what emerges. If a picture comes into your head as well as words, draw it or describe it.

2. Have your mother (the voice of your mother in your head) comment as if she has just finished reading the dialogue you've written. This commentary should be quite brief, just a sentence or two or a short paragraph.

3. Imagine your father's comment in the same way as your mother. Sometimes either one remains silent which is also significant. But if you can imagine what he might say, write it down.

4. Allow any other powerful influences from the past to comment on your money dialogue. It could be an ex-

partner, grandparent, best friend–anyone who influenced your relationship with money.

5. Finally, have God, your Higher Power, or your voice of inner wisdom comment on the dialogue you have written.

Your conversation with money will give you a more in-depth picture of how your life with money is going, what sticking points or conflicts are involved, and what your strengths and weaknesses are.

It will also give you a better handle on what influences from your past formed your money beliefs and finally, through your Higher Power or inner wisdom, this conversation will help you see what direction you need to move in, as well as any steps you can take or any attitudes you can adopt to evolve toward more harmony in your money life.

Conversations with money can (and should be) done again and again. Each time it will evolve more as your relationship with money becomes clearer and more conscious.

Now that you know what your relationship with money is right now, you can start working on building a different relationship to take into the future.

#2: Money Story Exercise

Your Money story is the starting point for your current money beliefs. It is quite possible that money wasn't openly talked about in your family.

It may have been yelled about or the topic quickly changed to avoid potential conflict. Without realising it you may have taken on your parents' behaviours and beliefs about money. Or, you may have rejected them, vowing never be like your mum or dad.

Once you understand the voices from the past, you can put them firmly where they belong, which is in your history, not your future. Their power over you will diminish.

It's only when we start to examine our beliefs that we discover which are working for us and which aren't.

It's time to start writing and let the story flow from all the thoughts and ideas you have written down as you went through Part One. Make sure one of your money stories includes your earliest memory of earning money.

Your beliefs start from childhood so think back to your early memories of money and see if they help identify the source of your money beliefs.

Be as detailed as you can be and aim for at least five stories, ranging from childhood through when you left home. As you finish each story ask yourself this question:

How has this experience affected the way I deal with money now?

To get you started, here's an example.

One summer when I was about 12, a friend called me and asked if I would help him with some gardening and mowing at a neighbour's house. The neighbour said she would pay him $20 and he would give me half. While my friend did the mowing, I weeded the flower beds that ran between the lawn and the fences. We worked for three hours and filled a couple of bins with weeds. When we were finished, he went to the door to ask to be paid. The lady was quite abrupt with him and said she wasn't satisfied with the job we had done, refused to pay, and slammed the door in his face. Once we got over our anger and disappointment, we realized there were several lessons from this experience. One was to work hard and do good quality work (which we thought we had done!) and the other was that people are not always fair. They don't always keep their word when it comes to money. I also realised I don't like gardening, but I do love mowing lawns!

To this day, fairness and keeping your word are two characteristics that I value extremely highly when working with people.

You might like to start by writing your story with pen and paper. If you think better that way, then go for it. If your iPad or tablet is your pen and paper of choice, then that is fine too.

You want to write your stories in a quiet, comfortable spot without distraction so that you can get into the flow and let the memories flood back.

It doesn't have to be grammatically correct and there is no word limit, this is all about you and crafting your own story, so do it your way and not anyone else's.

Once you have completed your stories you will find a number of beliefs that you have about money. Here are more questions to help add depth to your stories.

1. What did your parents (and other influential people in your childhood) teach you about money? This could be directly or indirectly.

    For example, the belief that money doesn't grow on trees is something you would have picked up indirectly from conversation or your parents' actions. Whereas the belief that it is important to save could have come directly from your parents teaching you how to allocate your pocket money.

2. Beliefs are interrelated, so what other beliefs support your original ones? What are the implications of this?

For example, if you believe you don't have enough money, the self–fulfilling prophecy kicks in and subconsciously you won't allow yourself to have enough, struggling to make ends meet. Even if you have enough, you still won't spend it.

3. Which of your money beliefs serve you well today?

   Our early beliefs become subconscious, so when we pull them to the front of our mind we can decide if they are working for us or not and, therefore, if we want to keep them. If they aren't, we can replace them with new ones.

4. From the beliefs you have identified, which ones would you like to replace?

   For example, if you were taught it wasn't polite to talk about money, you may find yourself having difficulty talking to clients about your fees. Is this working for you in your business?

5. What new beliefs would you like to have to replace the old?

   For example, it is fine to discuss money when appropriate to do so.

6. What do you think is standing in your way of making a start on transforming your beliefs about money?

Here are a few points to remember as you go through this process.

1. Beliefs appear to be real but are in fact of your own creation.

2. Beliefs are fed by emotion and emerge from some decision you made at some point in your life.

3. You can always change your mind.

4. When you look at the connection between the original decision and the view you now have, you need to acknowledge the impact that your assumption has had on your own life.

#3: What Is Holding You Back From Achieving Your Financial Dreams Exercise?

Write down on paper, not your computer or phone, a list of 20 things that you think are holding you back from achieving financial freedom.

Once you've done that, take a break, have a coffee, juice, or water, and take a short walk or some other activity to clear your head. When you come back have another look at the list.

Find a different coloured pen (markers are great for this) and cross everything off the list that is outside of your immediate control.

An example of this is the world economy. That is way out of your control (unless you are a national leader), so cross that off your list. If it's something to do with the climate, cross that off as well; we can't control the weather. Are you getting the picture?

How many items did that eliminate from your list?

Get another coloured pen and go through the list again, this time look for items that start with statements like:

I can reach my financial goals *when...* I finish my degree; I win the lotto; I get a better job; the kids leave home, etc. Look hard at these statements and decide if the *when* is valid. If not, cross it off, it's just an excuse.

You have to be ruthless and practical here!

The list should be getting quite a bit shorter by now. Keep going through it to refine, rephrase, and cross off until you are left with the five things holding you back but that **you can do something about now** to move towards financial freedom—to achieve your financial dreams.

Once you have these five things, start brainstorming solutions. Write down all of your ideas no matter how crazy!

The whole point of this exercise is to get you to expand your horizons and shift your locus of control from external (where you look outwards to others for solutions) to internal.

This is where you hold your future in your hands. You take responsibility and create the life you want, rather than just waiting for it to happen.

Maybe that statement makes you realize that you don't know what life it is that you want to live. Then it's time to do some dreaming! Imagine the life you'd love to create and set some goals to work towards your financial freedom. Little steps count.

Your final step is to take action—take one small step towards your financial dreams every day!

Let's move on to the exercises that are more directly related to you and your partner and your combined relationship with money.

#4: The Money Conversation Exercise

The Money Conversation with your partner is a very important step in understanding each other's relationship with money and how you can work together as a team.

Here are some guidelines on how to have a Money Conversation.

Don't view the money conversation as negative or scary. Look at it as a positive way to improve your relationship. The aim is to get a deeper understanding of how, as a couple, you can make the most of your different money beliefs and behaviours as well as what your non-negotiable might be.

Building a deeper understanding of your partner is what being in a relationship is all about, isn't it?

Yes, there will be some couples who end their relationship as a result of the conversation. If issues just can't be resolved between you, I suggest you seek external help and support from a trained Financial Therapist or Money Mentor. If that doesn't help, then it may well be the end of the road.

Don't let that stop you from having the conversation. If you have reservations about the outcome of the conversation, isn't it better to find out sooner rather than later? And before you potentially become a lot poorer too!

Don't just spring it on your partner; let them know you want to have a conversation about money and plan for it. Please don't use a scheduled date night and hijack it into a money conversation. If you have been struggling to talk about money, this is the worst thing you can do.

Set aside a time and place to have the conversation. If you are tired after a stressful day don't even attempt to have the money conversation. Find a favourite park or beach away from all other distractions where you can be open and talk to each other. Don't forget to turn off both of your phones and any notifications that might pop up on your watch. For the first few money conversations, I would suggest you leave the bottle of wine at home or have it after you've finished.

You can take notes as memory joggers for the next conversation if that's helpful, but not as the minutes of a committee meeting or to get into the 'You said...' conversation at another time, particularly if the conversation wasn't easy.

If the discussion starts to get heated or goes around in circles, stop. Take a break and agree to pick it up again another day. Don't leave it too long, agree to pick the conversation up in 24 or 48 hours. You don't want the negativity to fester for too long, it will either make the next conversation harder or you will continually put it off and never have it.

Some of the issues you bring up will have nothing to do with money; they will be about self-esteem, control, security, and so on. You need to listen carefully for the tone of the conversation to change.

Put yourself in your partner's shoes. Remember, men and women see money differently–they will have a different money story from you, and may well be a different money personality also.

Some of the questions you can discuss are:

- How did your parents handle money?

- Does debt scare you?

- Are you comfortable managing your own money?

- How was money handled in previous relationships? Did that work?

Discuss some different money scenarios and see how you would each handle the situation.

- What happens if one of us loses our job?

- How do you deal with an overdrawn bank account or credit card debt?

- What do you do when you want an overseas holiday?

- What about retirement? How are you going to plan for that?

- What are your investing styles, what do you want to invest in, and how much?

Don't expect to have the whole conversation at once; you may have to come back to it several times. Generally, one of you will find the conversation more difficult than the other. Watch for the signals of stress–stop the conversation, take a break, and either come back to it later or on another day. Decide when you will continue the conversation to make sure it happens.

Keep in mind, your goal is to strengthen and protect your relationship, so keep the lines of communication open, understand and respect each other's beliefs about money, and both should be prepared to compromise.

These difficult conversations make for a more peaceful future. You will have a much stronger foundation for your relationship once you get the money 'stuff' out of the way.

The best time to talk about money is before the conflict starts. But there are times when this may not be an option. I have met women who are scared to talk to their husbands about money because they just don't want to have to deal with the fallout. This is a serious situation to be in and way beyond the scope of this book. My best advice, if this is you, is to seek professional advice for your relationship as well as to find a Financial Therapist or Mentor/Coach who can discuss with you as an independent person.

Once you've had this conversation, you can move on to the other money conversations below. These aren't in any set order, they are simply guidelines of the key topics that you need to have discussions about in your relationship.

If you have found that your money conversation has gone around in circles and you are getting stuck, here is a good exercise for each of you to do individually to help you get those frustrations out of your system. The point of the exercise is to also find what is working well, so you can start by talk about those aspects rather than constantly getting stuck in the negatives, which is typically where we head first.

It's called the Money Dump (I wish I had come up with that term, but it comes from Scott and Bethany Palmer).

The Money Dump

Make space for two lists. The first list is all the *positive* aspects of your money relationship. Start each point with 'We'. Here are a few examples of prompts to get you thinking:

- What have you achieved financially as a couple?

- What are you proud of as a couple?

- Where are you aligned in your thinking about money?

The second list is everything that is *bugging* you about your financial relationship. Don't evaluate as you write–this is a money dump, time to get it all off your chest! Don't worry about blame or cause. Only YOU are going to see the list. Your sentences will start with 'We still...' or 'It bugs me when...'

Use bullet points or short sentences; you aren't writing a novel!

Once both of you have written your lists, take a break for an hour or so, then come back to your lists.

Take a fresh look at the list of *positives*. This shows what to continue to build on because you're doing some things well! Ask yourself, 'How did we make this happen?' Jot down a few notes as you talk about this in your money conversation.

Now have a look at the *bugging* list and prioritise the top two or three things; these are the ones that you would like to tackle over the next six months.

When deciding on the three things consider:

- Which are the most important to you?

- Which do you think are at the core of your financial communication problems?

It may take a few reviews to come up with the final list.

Once you have that list, jot down a few notes about why they bug you and what you think needs to be done about them.

Then ask yourself:

What is my part in this issue? Yes, you have played a part in this! This might be the hardest bit to admit.

What is my partner's part?

How would I like to see this issue resolved? What can both of you do? Make sure you don't just blame, or expect your partner to change, there are two of you in this relationship so make sure you take responsibility for your part here.

You don't have to share everything you have written in your Money Dump with your partner, the venting of frustrations is for your benefit, and probably not written in a way that would be received well by your partner, so feel free to keep that part to your selves. If you have both done the exercise you may be surprised to find you have similar answers about the frustrations, you just haven't been able to frame them in a way to be able to discuss them without friction occurring

Ideally, it's best if you can both do this exercise. But sometimes a reluctant partner won't join. In that case, it's still helpful for you to write everything down to help you focus on the positives. That's a great place to start talking with a reluctant partner. It also gives you a chance to look closely at what's bugging you and see what you can control and change on your own that will have an impact on the outcome.

Don't feel compelled to have a full-blown money conversation if your partner isn't ready. Actions often speak louder than words. Just quietly starting to make changes yourself can make a big difference. Over time, the money conversation will evolve.

There are several different communication techniques as well as a resource from the Gottman Institute on how to argue lovingly, you can use if you are finding it difficult to change your pattern of communication when talking about money. For the bonus workbook and exclusive readers free gifts please head to www.moneymentalist.com/bookbonus

The Household Banker Job Description

Someone has to be in charge of the money. One of you is probably already filling some of this role, you just don't see it as a 'job'. You have taken on the role whether you want to or not, it just happens. This can work well for some couples and for others it just doesn't, and that is where the problems begin. The reluctant household banker may not do a very good job, creating constant financial strife. Or maybe they're a little overzealous and you feel you have no say and no input into the decisions being made. Some household bankers feel the weight of the responsibility heavily and it can cause them quite a bit of stress, especially if they have a partner who is a happy money delegator who has delegated all financial responsibility.

If we lived in a perfect world, this would be the job description for your household banker. Ideally, this will be the one of you who has the best skills for the job.

1. Takes responsibility for making sure the bills get paid on time. Finds any discounts you may be entitled to for early payment or paying upfront instead of monthly.

2. Makes sure the expenses are reviewed regularly. Depending on your financial situation, this might be weekly, monthly or quarterly. This ensures you aren't overpaying for services like phone, power, and insurance.

3. Monitors your Money Plan and updates the other on your financial date nights.

4. Makes sure any backwards movement, like a sudden increase in fuel prices or the annual insurances, is accounted for and adjustments are made as needed. Sometimes this occurs when we change habits, take some time off unexpectedly, or when life just happens. You'll want to pick up on these things early before it gets out of control. Comes up with a creative plan to get back on track. Most importantly, discusses it with the rest of the family to make sure everyone does their part.

Go through the job description together and decide who has the best skill set and/or desire for the task.

Who is your household banker? _______________________________

You could swop this role around so not just one of you is responsible all the time. Discuss what that might look like for you as a couple—what's the best schedule for swopping, how will the transition happen, and what tools will you use for money management? Swopping the role around also helps share the mental load and brings your money personality styles closer together if you are opposites.

We all know we don't live in a perfect world, so start with steps one and two and build up to the rest of the job description as you become more confident.

If this sounds a bit formal, it's meant to be. Managing your money is a serious business. It's a very important part of your life.

Don't Delegate Your Financial Responsibilities

'I'm not good with money.'

'I don't have to worry about money, my partner handles it all.'

'I trust my partner completely when it comes to our money.'

Comments like this are a real concern in a relationship, particularly if the person making these comments is a Money Avoider personality. If you are both Avoiders then nothing will get done! One of you will have to move towards the Hoarder personality.

Handing over total control of your finances to your partner is never a good idea. This is compounded when you then abdicate all responsibility and don't want to know what is happening.

Trust is a wonderful thing and the basis for any relationship. However, if you are going to hand over control, you need to make sure that you still know what's happening, keep an eye on bank accounts, ask questions, and if your partner wants to talk money, then listen!

When you have your money conversations be aware of what you are delegating and where you could be abdicating your responsibility.

If at some point the going gets tough (financially, I mean), and you continue to 'not want to know', you are putting huge stress on your partner and potentially your relationship as well. It's hard for your partner to tell you what's happening if you don't want to know, let alone tell you that you may have to change your lifestyle because money has hit a bad patch. Or, even worse, you continue in blind faith believing that 'things will be fine' and you happily remain in your bubble, while they continue to carry the burden and feel unsupported.

I recall meeting with a couple who had a great relationship. They talked about everything... except money. He managed all the money and she had a credit card she used frequently. She didn't want to talk about money; she trusted her partner completely so felt she didn't need to know the ins and outs of their finances. When I asked her partner how he felt about their money management, he said he was constantly stressed about money. The 100% responsibility weighed heavily on his shoulders. He felt he couldn't talk to his partner about any concerns, even if he wanted to, as she would just brush them aside. He felt alone in that aspect of their relationship. When his partner heard this, she was shocked; he had never voiced this before. She was also upset that her attitude towards money was causing her partner so much stress. They realised that they needed to make some changes. We implemented the financial date night. She was now open to wanting to learn more about the household finances, so we started gently by just looking at the fixed costs—mortgage, phone, power, etc., and then they moved on to their discretionary income. Together, over a few months, they put some boundaries around household spending. They also put some goals in place, so they had a reward structure built in for changing their spending. They began with a great relationship and moved into an even stronger, more supportive one.

When Do You Merge Your Money?

To merge or not to merge, that is the question.

When my mum and dad got married (over 60 years ago now), it was automatic–the woman changed her name and they set up joint bank accounts. It's just what you did. It wasn't until the 1960s in the US that a woman could even get an account in her own name.

Now, with the high rate of relationship breakup and people wanting to remain 'independent' a lot of couples are opting to keep their name and their finances their own.

There are more choices around merging or not and some don't feel compelled to merge their finances just because they're in a long-term relationship. Many couples still ultimately want to fully merge their finances. Merging is often easier to manage; you don't end up double paying or spending more than you realise.

That's the practical aspect but it's also about trust. We trust our partners to care for us physically and emotionally, so why don't we trust them with our money as well? This is possible when you have good communication about money, a joint vision, as well as setting really clear and focused goals for your relationship. But you don't have to do it on day one, you can always decide to merge when you both feel that it's beneficial and you're ready.

The first step is what I call a partial merge. It's a bit like when you first go flatting after you leave home, and you have four or five people in a flat. You open up a flat account and the rent money goes in, plus a bit for extras like cleaning products. A partial merge is exactly the same, you both contribute to an account to meet your joint expenses and everything else remains separate.

This is a good place to start the process of merging your finances. You get to test the waters and see how you both behave with money. You'll find out where the niggles are, what works well, and what doesn't.

For a partial merge to work well, you do have to talk to each other about money and how you are going to structure the joint account. You'll want to talk through questions like:

- What expenses will be paid from the joint account? If we think about our flat account example, it will be rent, power, insurance, food staples, cleaning products, internet, streaming services, entertainment, children's expenses, and anything else that you decide are joint expenses.

- What is not part of the joint account? Are gym subscriptions joint or separate? What if one of you wants to eat organically and the other doesn't worry about that?

- How much will each contribute to the joint account and when?

- What happens if someone can't afford their portion?

Dealing with the scenario of unequal income can be tricky. There are several different approaches. The obvious is 50/50, which is fine if the difference in income isn't too great. This can be tough if there is a significant difference in income as that can leave one of you with no money at the end of the month and the other with plenty which can cause resentment. Another option is to apportion the expenses based on income. If you earn double what your partner does, you contribute double to the joint account. The main point is to decide on an approach or formula that is going to work for you, your lifestyle, and your relationship.

How long you stay in the partial merge scenario is totally up to you. Some couples remain this way permanently and others move to a full merge.

When you start to think about major financial decisions, like buying a home together and starting a family, you should have already worked through the money behaviours from Chapter 8. You will know which of you is the Spender or Hoarder, for example, what each other's financial situation and earnings are, and you are setting joint financial goals. Now is the time to start merging fully and use the power of combined thinking to achieve your goals.

Before you consider merging, make sure you have worked through the reasons not to merge. If you are unsure about any of the points below, hold back and wait.

1. Don't merge your finances until you know your partner's full financial situation. If they come to the relationship with bad credit or significant debt, this can affect your own and joint credit rating. You need to know exactly what the situation is and have a plan on how to deal with it before you merge. This may mean running credit checks on each other (you are in this together, so don't just pick on one of you). It might mean taking some advice to restructure debt if that's appropriate. It also means your partner can share their financial situation without feeling ashamed or inadequate, so your empathy and listening skills are important to enable that to happen.

2. Don't merge your finances until you have set some boundaries around spending. If one of you is a Spender and the other is a Saver and you merge your finances, resentment can build very quickly on both sides without boundaries (i.e. a budget) in place.

3. Don't merge your finances until you've had the money conversation. We all have financial baggage. Whether it comes from our parents or past relationships, until you and your partner have worked through this, it may be best to not merge your finances completely. This process can take several years to work through.

4. Do not merge your finances if your partner has addictive behaviour. This could be shopping, alcohol, or another type of addiction. A relationship like this needs serious counselling to work through the addiction issues before you even contemplate sharing a bank account or credit card.

The key message is this: don't feel that you have to combine your finances as soon as you have entered into a long-term relationship. There are stepping stones along the way.

Having Your Own Money

Whether you are fully merged or partially, it's very important, and more so for women (according to Olivia Mellan, our expert on money and relationships), that you have some separate money.

The cynical say that women need to have separate money to protect themselves should the relationship fail.

Olivia Mellan, on the other hand, says it's important for women to have separate money to give them their own sense of identity.

Whatever the reason, both of you need to have 'play money' of your own that you can do with what you like. This becomes even more important if you are a stay-at-home parent who has been used to having your own money. If you are planning a family and looking at your money plan, make sure you still have play money going into the bank account of the stay-at-home parent. It can be humiliating and a knock to your self-esteem if you have to ask your partner for money to go out for a coffee with friends, particularly if you are already feeling stressed and sleep-deprived with a young baby.

How much that is will depend on your circumstances and whether you are partially or fully merged. You need to do the 'merge or not' exercise first, then how much goes into your play money will drop out of that exercise.

I worked with a couple who had fully merged their finances. They have been married for about 15 years and had a couple of children. When I first started working with them they didn't have separate money. The husband (who was the Hoarder) got grumpy every month when he looked at the finances and complained about how much she spent on nails and going out for coffee with her friend. It wasn't that they couldn't afford it, he was focused on debt reduction and felt she was 'wasting' money. To remove this niggly conflict, his wife opened up a bank account of her own, and we did one transfer a month that covered the nails and girl time. Hubby was happy, even though it was the same amount as before. It was how he viewed the money that was the issue, not the amount.

The Financial Date Night

It's all well and good having all these conversations and putting all these plans in place, but what then? How do you keep the momentum going? This is where the financial date night comes in. I often tell clients to run their household finances like a well-run business.

The key characteristics of a well-run business are:

- Someone is in charge of the money.
- There's a plan for what they want to achieve.
- They measure and review results to make sure they are on track.

The financial date night helps you achieve all of these things. They keep the lines of communication open so you are both on the same page, heading in the same direction.

What is a financial date night? It's when you allocate a set time to sit down together and have a planned conversation and discussion about your finances. It doesn't have to be in the evening, it can be any time of the day that works for you. The key thing is that it's regular—set aside an hour or so once a month. Make sure it's in the diary and is non-negotiable. A bit of planning is required here to make sure it's not going to clash with kids' events or your commitments.

I can hear the Money Avoiders and Spenders going, 'Good grief, I can't think of anything worse than a date to talk about money'. The Hoarders will be excited at the prospect of pulling out the financial spreadsheet and going through every last item of expenditure over the past month! If your date night turns into an argument (as the first few may well do), don't give up. Take some time out, postpone to another day if you have to, but come back to the problem when you are both calm. Don't let the month slip by; reschedule for a couple of days ahead, not next week!

Numbers are an important part of your financial date night. What else do you talk about on a financial date night?

You plan for the future, short-term plans, and some longer-term plans. Once you've got the number crunching and the bill-paying out of the way, that's when the fun part of the evening starts because you start to look ahead. You start to look forward.

You get to look at questions like:

- What have we achieved in the last month or the last quarter?

- What does our personal balance sheet (what we own and what we owe) look like now?

- Are we getting ahead of where we thought we were going to be?

- Are our debts going down?

- Is our savings going up?

- Do we have a bit of surplus that enables us to do something fun as a family that we hadn't planned on?

- It's important to be spontaneous too!

Talk about your shared vision for your relationship. Where do you want to go, how are you going to get there, and where are you right now along the pathway?

The end of your date night should always end with a cuddle, not an argument. If it's going to end with an argument, stop and pick it up another time.

Financial dates take practice, but you'll get the hang of it, experience how it draws you closer and breeds more trust, and start to look forward to and enjoy having a financial date night with your partner.

As one client said to me, the conversations with her partner had all been transactional. Who's picking the kids up from school? Have you paid the power bill? Can you add cat food to the shopping list? What she loved about the financial date night was that they got to talk about the really important things about their lives: their family and their relationship. It changed their relationship significantly over time; they felt much closer and connected.

At the core of all of this is *trust*. When we fall in love, we are placing a huge amount of trust in that person to look after us, both emotionally and physically. We get into the car with our partner and trust them to get us to our destination safely. We may bring up children together, trusting our partners to support us in the parenting role. So, why do we often find it so difficult to trust those we love with our money? To talk about it openly and share it together?

All of these steps are building blocks in a happy money marriage. They may seem a bit overwhelming and a bit too hard at first. If you don't know where to start, I suggest you start with a financial date night; keep it short and simple and get used to talking about money together in a positive way. Once you have practised that a few times you will be better equipped to tackle some of the more difficult aspects of your relationship and how money works in it.

Finally, remember that the goal is to nurture your money together, plan for it together, spend it together, and enjoy it together.

What's Next?

Once you have the day-to-day finances working for you, you're having great money conversations, the date night is going well, and you're feeling good about where you are, the next step is the fun part. This is building a money plan and starting to build your wealth (whatever that means for you). A caveat here: wealth doesn't always mean money, it might be having enough money so you can work less and spend more time with the family, for example. Check in with your values to see what's important to you and what your 'enough' is.

You are bound to have a few blips along the way. It's important to understand how change happens so you know what to expect over the next few months as your awareness of your money grows.

Sometimes change can happen quickly when something drastic happens and we are forced to change overnight. Unfortunately, it tends to be negative events like accidents and illnesses that bring about this kind of change. But when we want to make a change ourselves, it is slower and there is a process. In the next chapter, we'll talk about how to engage this process of change.

CHAPTER 14

IMPLEMENTING CHANGE

By now you've had a very good look at yourself, your relationship with money, and how you behave with money. Both individually and with your partner. You will have recognised some aspects that you are happy with and some that you aren't. The next question is: how do you change what you aren't happy with?

The answer is **slowly.**

Like any change, if you try and do it too quickly you will fall flat on your face.

As my mentor, David Krueger, says, '**Change is not an event, it's a process**'. This is an important concept to bear in mind and keep coming back to.

I see too many people setting themselves up to fail. Say, for example, you have had a credit card balance of $5,000 for the past couple of years. You decide you are going to pay it back in three months. Unless you have had a windfall gain, like a bonus or tax refund, it isn't very likely you are going to achieve that just by cutting out a coffee or two a week. You are going to have to be hard on yourself–which you probably won't enjoy so you likely won't do it for the three months. Then you'll feel bad and beat yourself up about being useless at managing your money and getting out of debt. So, you go shopping to cheer yourself up and you are back at square one! Sound like a familiar story?

It was probably a lot of small decisions that got you into the position you're in now. Use the same process to make changes.

Before you start doing anything different, take a close look at what you are doing now. What are the small decisions you make every day that impact your money? What habits have you identified that you can tweak a little that will make a difference in the long term?

Do you eat out more than you eat at home? Do you treat everyone when you go out socially? Are your children using you as the Bank of Mum and Dad?

By taking a step back, you will see quite a few areas of life where you could make small changes to get to where you want to be.

Pick just one of them. Don't try to change everything all at once, it's overwhelming!

For example, if you eat out four nights a week, cut that back to two or three. If you were to average what you spend each time you go out and apply that directly to your credit card, how quickly could you repay the debt? Even if it took 12 months, that is still better than your current position, so stick with it and be proud of yourself.

What if that just doesn't work? Then try something else. You may not get things right the first time around–the key is to not give up. Go back to the drawing board and do something else.

Everything we do is to fulfil our needs. Unmet needs cause frustration. We often use financial strategies to meet needs that could be fulfilled by non-financial strategies. So, if your current strategy isn't working, look at the underlying need, then try a different strategy.

By identifying the need you are wanting to fulfil, you will be able to adapt your spending more easily. This will ensure your needs are met and you have more money in your pocket at the end of the week.

Keep reminding yourself, change is not an event, it's a process. Small decisions add up over time, whether it's the decision to have the chocolate muffin every day (and five years later you've gained 10kg) or you buy lots of little things and have debt.

Make a conscious decision to make small changes in your life and then just do it!

This all sounds very straightforward. But if it was easy, everyone would be perfect and sadly, we aren't. Change is hard. We all have comfort zones, and we like to stay in them, even if they are uncomfortable (so long as they're less uncomfortable than the alternative).

Comfort Zones And Change

What do comfort zones and change have to do with each other? I hadn't given it much thought either. It was only when I was doing my New Money Story Mentor training with David Kruger that I realised the importance of recognising your comfort zones and just how difficult they are to change.

We use the term 'comfort zone' frequently, but what does it mean?

A comfort zone is a familiar pattern of behaviour. The process happens gradually, but once in place, it resists change.

We have comfort zones in all areas of our lives, from how we think to how we act and what we do. For example, procrastinating, working under pressure, and creating a crisis can all be comfort zones. It's predictable, automatic, and we know the outcome.

Try changing your morning routine. Hold your toothbrush in a different hand or take a different route to work. Monitor how you feel and how strong the pull is to be back in your comfort zone.

A comfort zone is like a thermostat, we set the temperature we want (the comfort zone) and if there is a variation up or down, the thermostat kicks in and brings us back to where we were.

We have comfort zones around everything: our weight, our money, and our habits. We will return to our comfort zone even if it harms us because it's familiar and we know the outcome.

Think about the lottery winners who spend or lose their winnings and return to their previous situation or worse. A combination of their beliefs and their comfort zones pull them back to where they started.

The same applies to people who lose significant weight (think about contestants on reality weight loss TV shows). They lose the weight and then gain it back, sometimes more than they lost originally.

Why does this happen? Well, the money changed, or their body changed, but their mindset didn't. They returned to the familiar: their comfort zone.

But don't despair, you *can* change; you can break out of your comfort zones or habits and improve or form new ones. Moving out of your comfort zone is going to feel uncomfortable initially because it's a change in routine. The more uncomfortable you feel, the more you are changing.

A comfort zone is an unconscious thermostat; it remains in the back of your mind. When it moves to consciousness, you can reprogramme yourself.

Often the methods used to make change are contrary to how the brain and mind work. So even if you know the change will benefit you, you still don't change.

Let's think of changing your habits in terms of an equation.

Event + Response = Outcome

Put another way: every outcome you experience in life is the result of how you respond to an event.

It's not *what* happens, but how we respond that makes the difference.

If you don't like the outcome, you have two things you can focus on:

1. The event
2. Your response

For example, imagine someone cuts you off in traffic and you get angry. For the rest of the day, you are in a bad mood. It's the idiot in the other car's fault that you are in a bad mood. In other words, you've decided that the event is to blame.

Change your *response* to get the result you want. You can't change the event but you can control your response. Don't let the other motorist wind you up and ruin your day. How do you do that? One way I take control of the moment is to put on some music I enjoy and sing loudly while continuing my drive. You could choose to be grateful that the other driver didn't cause a collision with you. You could take deep breaths and ground yourself in the present moment. You could just think happy thoughts and smile instead!

YOU can either *create* Your reality–get cut off in traffic and smile and carry on with your day, deciding to be happy.

Or you can *agree* to it–get home tired and grumpy as a result of a bad day because you got cut off in traffic.

As you work through the process of challenging your comfort zone, be aware of a couple of important points.

1. You will create ways to go back to your old habits. Why? As you end a habit and begin a new one, you will be confused, maybe even distressed. Think about the last time you tried to change your eating habits; you often craved the food you were trying to give up–it can be stressful.

2. Change-Back Pressure: never underestimate the pressure friends and family may exert for you to stay where you are and not change. You are moving them out of their comfort zone in their relationship with you, and whilst many will support your decision to change, just as many will be pressuring you to not.

The Cycle of Change

The second point is important and often underestimated when you are trying to make changes to your own life. This is why it's so important to have someone in your camp supporting you and helping you to move through the cycle of change.

A model developed by Don Kelley and Daryl Conner in the mid-70s called The Emotional Cycle of Change is a very useful model to know and apply, as it's still very relevant today.

This model will help you understand the ups and downs you may feel once you decide to change.

The cycle has five stages, as shown in Figure 1 below.

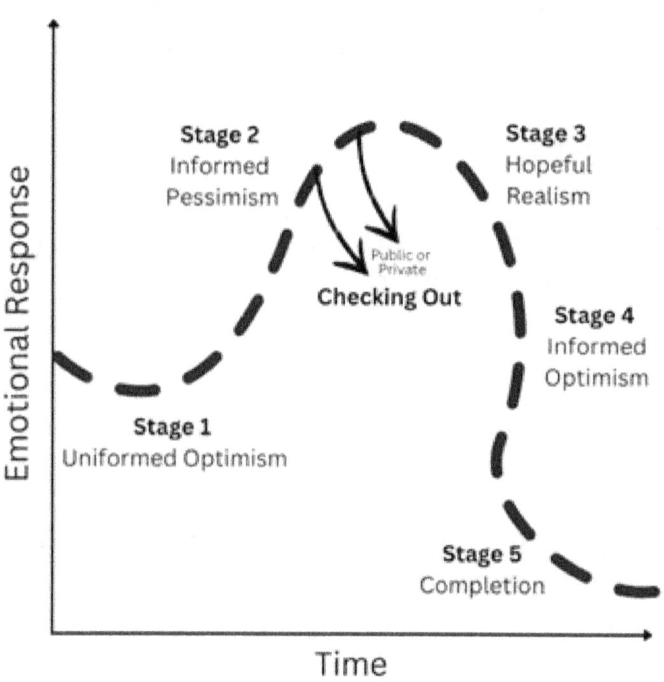

Figure 1 – The Emotional Cycle of Change

Stage 1: Uninformed Optimism. In this stage, you have decided to take on a new challenge, and as you don't know what's involved yet, you are optimistic about the outcome.

Stage 2: Informed Pessimism. Oh dear, the going is getting tough. You have a much clearer idea about the challenge you have taken on and it's getting hard. There's a strong temptation to quit and return to the familiar comfort zone. Your coach or accountability buddy is really important to you at this time; they are the ones who will be there to get you through, keep you moving forward, and help you not listen to the voice in your head or your friends who are telling you to quit.

Between this stage and stage three is where most people give up and revert to their old comfort zone. There doesn't seem to be a light at the end of the tunnel and you feel despair. Knowing that you are in this stage and that it's only a phase gives you the strength and impetus to keep going and break through into stage three.

Stage 3: Hopeful Realism. Things are looking up, life is getting a little easier, and you are starting to see the results of your actions. The goal is starting to look attainable, your old comfort zone is falling away like an old skin, and the new you is starting to emerge.

Stage 4: Informed Optimism. There is no holding you back at this stage. Success is in sight and you know with just a bit more pushing you will get there.

Stage 5: Completion. You have done it! Goal achieved, enjoy the success and savour the moment, then move on to the next challenge and let the cycle begin again.

To have a really impactful change, there is another area that you need to check in with: are my beliefs in alignment with my values?

As a Money Mentor, I listen to and learn from as many different experts and perspectives about money as I can. I attended one of Dr John De Martini's talks on wealth, and I'll share what I learned from him about belief alignment and values.

Creating wealth isn't just about changing money behaviours; you need to go much deeper than that and explore your beliefs and core values. This is what you have been working on so far as you read (and do the exercises) in this book.

If you ask a room full of people how many of them want to be financially free, most of them will raise their hands. When you ask the same room to put their hand up if they are financially free, very few will. Why is this?

I love the way Dr De Martini puts it: 'We fantasize about the lifestyle of being financially independent but have the desire to spend money, not to create wealth'. These are two very different sides of the coin.

So why can so few people seem to create financial wealth? According to the research Dr De Martini has done, if creating wealth isn't in your top three values it probably isn't going to happen for you.

The first thing you need to do is work out what your core values are. On the Dr De Martini website, https://drdemartini.com/values/, you will find an excellent tool to help you do this. There are plenty of other options as well, just be careful you don't go too far down the rabbit hole by trying too many—you will just end up confused!

You will become wealthy in whatever your highest value is. For example, if family is your highest value, then you will nurture your family, be the best parent that you can be, and quite probably sacrifice your own wealth creation for your family. Your wealth will come from the love and respect that your family has for you, which will hopefully flow into them looking after you financially if you can't do it for yourself.

So, what is your highest value? If it isn't wealth, then you need to nurture whatever your highest value is and your wealth will flow from that.

Do You Want To Be Rich *Or* Wealthy?

It's an interesting question, as many people think they're the same thing, but they're not. There is quite a distinction between the two.

The question 'Are you rich or are you wealthy'? is explored in Paul Sullivan's book *The Thin Green Line*. When Sullivan interviewed Michael Sonnenfeldt, (Founder of the TIGER21 network for high-net-worth individuals) he put it like this: 'My perception is many people who are not wealthy, they think the key to getting rich is making a lot of money but look at all the movie stars and athletes who have made endless amounts of money and are dirt-poor. They make $10-15 million a year and they get to 45 years old, and they are flat broke'.

He continues, 'What's seen is the money they made, but what's unseen is the choices that they've made. It's what allows them to continue to be wealthy (or not)'. This is the clincher–'The issue is not in any way to diminish the success you're enjoying. The issue is to look at the implications of the choices you have made relative to the success you have had'.

What does this mean? Being wealthy is different from being rich. Rich is a number, and as the Great Depression in the 1930s and the GFC in 2008 showed, being rich didn't equate to being financially secure. The rich are those who drive expensive cars, have huge debt, and are 'living the life' until it all comes crashing down and they realise they have nothing to fall back on.

Being wealthy, on the other hand, is having more money than you need, so you know you can do all the things you want to do. Being wealthy isn't the exclusive right of a high-profile person or professionals. Being wealthy can apply to anyone from any walk of life who is prepared to make some tough choices about what they choose to have now and what they choose to delay to reach their financial goals. Being wealthy is the living and breathing definition of what our Money Master personality is.

Klontz highlights a few of the key points that came out of his research for the book Mind Over Money he and Sullivan (a financial psychologist) cowrote to study what made the difference between the rich and the wealthy. The stereotype of the wealthy portrayed in the media is not, in many cases, who the wealthy really are.

Net worth (or your wealth) is what you hold onto, not how much you spend. What the wealthy actually spend (according to the Klontz research) is not what is portrayed on TV, so it's very easy to self-sabotage your wealth creation by doing what you see the wealthy do on TV to be like them, leaving yourself poor.

The research also highlighted that the wealthy have different money scripts (beliefs); they are low on money avoidance beliefs and high on money status beliefs.

The wealthy also have a high internal locus of control–they take more responsibility for their actions, for what is working in their lives and what isn't.

So, if you want to be wealthy as opposed to rich, stop focusing on the stereotypes of what you think wealth is and start working on your own beliefs and behaviours.

Now that we have established that wealth is the way to go, you need to build your financial awareness, which is understanding and being in control of how you earn, spend, save, and grow your money.

It's about knowing what's coming into your bank account each payday and making smart decisions all the time about where that money goes.

Ultimately, it's a change in the way you think about money–rather than functioning on autopilot. It's about making considered decisions with a bigger financial picture in mind.

Of course, the basic rule here is to spend less than you earn–it's hard to build wealth otherwise!

Five Steps To Building Your Wealth

1. Have a clear financial objective

When I ask new clients about their financial goals, many times I'll get a vague answer that involves paying off debt or owning their home freehold. Rarely can anyone paint me a detailed picture of what their ultimate financial future looks like.

Being able to visualise your goals is the first step to realising them. If you don't have a clear idea of where you want to end up financially, I encourage you to spend time getting clear on what you want.

Consider that since wealth means different things to different people, your partner might have different goals than you. It's important to understand and respect one another's goals, and to do your best to achieve what's important to both parties.

2. Maximise your earnings

For some of us, income from employment is the main building block for establishing and building wealth. So it makes sense to try and maximise your earning potential from your employer! While negotiating a pay rise is an obvious way to increase your income, here are other strategies to consider as well.

- Join a retirement savings scheme. In many countries, your employer will contribute to this as part of your salary package.

- Get the most out of your workplace benefits. Find out what benefits your employer provides that could help you save a few extra dollars each month. A common example is subsidised health insurance. Some large employers have negotiated group discounts on all sorts of other things too, from gym memberships to travel benefits.

- Keep up to date. Take every relevant training opportunity that comes up within your organisation. Being highly trained will make you a more valuable employee, which is a great position to be in when your annual salary review comes around. By showing an interest in developing your skills, you're also more likely to be considered for promotion.

- If your choice is to use your business to maximise your income, then make sure you have a well-run, profitable business. Find out if you have a business that you can sell or a business that generates a strong income stream. Your business strategy will be different depending on the end game.

- If investment is how you plan to maximise your earnings, you need to understand what you are investing in, the risks as well as the rewards. Have a good team of advisers around you that you trust and respect.

3. Spend wisely

If you concentrate on maximising your income, it follows that you should also ensure you're getting the best possible value for every dollar you spend.

Having a Money Plan will help you keep track of how much you're spending each month and give you a good indication of whether you're living within your means. It doesn't need to be complicated—a simple Excel spreadsheet with columns for each month's income and outgoings will do the trick.

Keeping a closer eye on your outgoings will also help you focus on getting maximum value for money when you spend.

Spending wisely is spending consciously, you know what is important to you and you focus on that. You don't waste money, but you are meeting all of your needs. This is different from a frugalist who can deprive themselves of things now that are important to them for the sake of their future self.

4. Get into the habit of saving

You might have put off saving in the past because of a tight budget—a common example is young families that have a relatively new mortgage and a single income.

Successful saving is as much about habit as it is about dollars. If you can only afford to save $10 a week, that's great! Don't decide it's not enough to start—get your savings effort started anyway. Regularly review your household spending to see whether you are wasting money on low-value items. Good examples are lotto tickets and bought lunches. If you are spending on these things, try allocating that amount to your savings account instead.

Once every six months, review your weekly savings amount and think about whether you could increase it just a little over the next six months. Again, even if it's only an extra $10, do it and feel proud!

5. Focus on paying off debt

If you are planning to own your own home, mortgage debt is inevitable. However, a mortgage is a very different type of debt to the kind that's lurking on your credit card, car loan, or hire purchase.

While some personal debt may be necessary to finance major expenses (for example, a car or student loan), always make sure you have a plan for paying that debt back as quickly as possible before you take it on.

Beware if you have a 'revolving credit' overdraft facility on your mortgage. It can be very tempting to splurge on an overseas holiday or a new lounge suite, instead of focussing on getting the overdraft facility down to $0.

One of my favourite methods for reducing debt is Dave Ramsey's snowball effect. You can find out more about this in the workbook http://www.moneymentalist.com/bookbonus

Build A Money Plan Instead Of A Budget

I have used the term budget up to this point as it's a term we all understand, but to be honest, it's not a word that I like to use.

How many times have you tried a budget and failed? Why have you failed?

Budgets were developed by accountants. It's called the 'cashflow model' and it measures what comes in (your income), then subtracts what goes out (your expenses). And with a bit of luck, you'll have some left over, which is your savings. If you have no savings or are spending more than you earn, the model says you cut back expenses, which is a budget. The 'B-word' really has negative connotations, doesn't it? It makes you feel like you're being controlled and you can't have all of those nice things in life that are important to you. That's why budgets don't work long-term. They are great if you are deep in the mire. But if you just want to improve your financial position, they aren't so great.

Building a Money Plan looks at a budget from a completely different perspective. A Money Plan is a lifestyle tool, it's part of your self-care, just like looking after your health. Like a budget, it also looks at the source of your income and how you can increase what you've got coming in. There are many different ways that you can do this. You can sell your time for money, i.e.

a job or freelance work. You can look at what surrounds you—stuff or your house. Airbnb is a classic example of using your resources to increase your income. You might have some spare time where you can teach others to do something for hire. What do your friends ask to borrow from you all the time? Maybe someone else would like to hire that from you. Exploring ways to increase your income is always the starting point of a Money Plan.

Let's look at the other side: what goes *out*? Let's think about this differently. This is the key differentiator between a budget and a money plan. Everything we do is to fulfil a need. In our society, we tend to use money to fulfil those needs when maybe we could use non-financial means or spend less to meet those needs.

One major problem is that our society now says that everything is a need! That's one of the biggest mind shifts you'll make when you build a Money Plan. Look at what you are spending now and, line by line, ask *why* you are spending that money. Why do you have the gym sub? Is it really because you want the equipment at the gym that you can't get anywhere else? Is it the social connection of meeting friends? Why don't you go for a walk in the park instead? Are you seeing what you truly value? Start analyzing how you're using your money by asking why and then start making different choices.

Identify the actual need, look at the strategy that you are currently using, and then assess whether it's the best strategy or if can you find a better one. When you start looking at building a Money Plan from this perspective, expanding your resources (your income) and meeting your needs with good solid strategies, you will be amazed at the shift that can happen. My clients are doing amazing things, going from being in a negative situation to having savings every week. Guess what? They're happy. They don't feel deprived; they are loving life. Build a Money Plan, don't build a budget, and you'll enjoy it too.

I always ask my clients, 'What has changed for you now that you have a money plan?'

One of the most unusual answers I've heard is 'We're eating less sugar'. I was curious to know more. 'Well', they said, 'as we were reviewing our spending, we noticed we were rewarding our children with sugary treats for doing chores and behaving well. We decided to ask them what they wanted as their reward and they wanted a trip to the park to have a picnic as a family. What they wanted was time, not sugar'. You never know what is going to happen or change when you build a Money Plan instead of a budget.

By the way, if you are telling yourself that you can never manage your money like this because you just don't have the skills, you are wrong.

Managing your money is a learned skill, it just isn't taught very well. We start learning about money from our immediate family. If your parents weren't good at managing money or never talked about it, you probably didn't pick up the good habits you need to get ahead financially.

Unless you set about learning the skills yourself, either by asking questions or learning through bitter experience, you're probably still wandering around in the dark wondering why you aren't where you thought you would be by now.

How Gratitude Helps You Manage Your Money Better

We touched on gratitude in Chapter 4 when we looked at spending money and your emotions. I want to expand on it here as I think it's pretty cool.

Is it really as simple as counting your blessings? Research seems to say that yes, a mindset of gratitude helps you handle your money better due to increased patience. Not only that, but gratitude also helps increase your happiness and decrease the likelihood you'll succumb to temptation.

We know money is emotional. And many emotions can have the effect of making us spend more. It's a bit like comfort eating when we're upset–when we're upset or angry, the temptation is to spend more. So it's really good news that a positive emotion like gratitude (and one that we can easily evoke in ourselves) positively impacts how we spend.

How did the researchers come to this conclusion? The study had a group of 75 participants. The purpose of the study was to test financial self-control, or in other words, the ability to delay gratification.

The participants were placed in one of three emotional states: grateful, happy, or neutral. They were then told they could have $54 now or $80 in 30 days. If you do the calculation, that's a 48% return on their money! That's very good! But money isn't about maths–it's about emotion.

Those in the happy and neutral group showed a strong preference for having $54 now. Behavioural economics tells us this is quite a normal response. The temptation to have something immediately is very strong, and we don't tend to think about the maths unless it's a great deal more that we'll receive later.

However, those in the gratitude group were much more likely to wait for the $80 in 30 days, and the greater gratitude they felt, the longer they were prepared to wait.

An important point to note here is that just feeling happy wasn't enough to delay gratification–it was the *specific feeling of gratitude.* This result is interesting not just in terms of money behaviours, but it also has implications for obesity and smoking.

The next question has to be: How do we cultivate this emotion of gratitude, particularly when the temptation to spend our money is at its greatest?

Keeping a gratitude journal works for many people. Each day, jot down two or three things that you're grateful for. It could be as simple as being grateful that your train was on time, that your baby smiled at you, or that your teenager said actual words to you instead of grunting.

From a practical perspective, when you want to spend money, put yourself in a state of gratitude When the impulse strikes, or if you are in your usual routine of shopping whether for groceries or anything else, take a 10-second break and think about two or three things you're grateful for. Quite often, being grateful for what you already have is enough to reduce the desire for more.

IT'S A WRAP!

Everything you've read and the exercises you've done leads you to this question: As a couple, what would it be like to have easy, uplifting conversations about money, so you can build a solid financial base for you and your children?

You may well have started this journey like many couples–you didn't talk about money, or maybe you yelled about it, which isn't very constructive. Or on the other end of the spectrum, maybe you avoided talking about it or never finished the conversation. You blamed each other for spending the money 'It isn't me, it's you.' You feel like you are drifting along financially not making any real long-term plans and hoping for the best.

But by digging a bit deeper I have found that couples avoid talking about money because they are worried about causing an argument or hurting each other. They start to keep financial secrets from each other. Maybe a secret bank account, or a new credit card, and they don't tell their partner about it.

Learning to understand your own *and* your joint relationship with money and how to communicate effectively within your relationship is a bit like climbing a mountain. When you stand at the bottom looking up, it looks unassailable. But as you start to climb, just by focusing on the next step, you make your way up. You may have to navigate the odd boulder along the way, but as you get fitter the journey gets easier. When you reach the top and look at the amazing view and where you have come from, you will wonder why you didn't do it sooner.

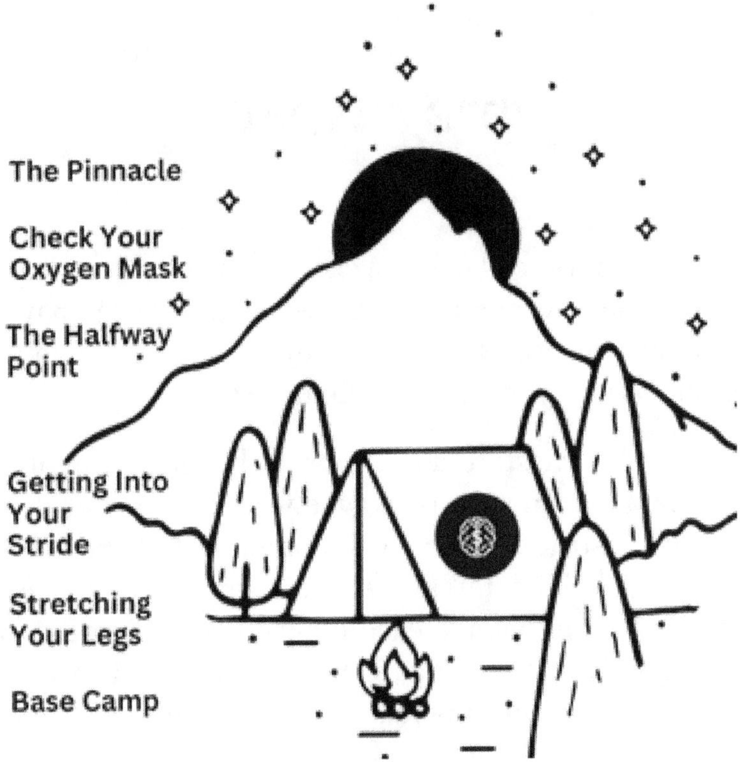

Figure 2 - Climbing the mountain

You have started to climb the mountain.

When you picked up this book, maybe you weren't even at **Base Camp.** You had no idea about your relationship with money, let alone how to fit it together with your partner. And you had no idea what was ahead of you in this journey. What you *did* know was that you needed to do something because you just weren't on the same page about your money. You don't want your relationship to deteriorate, so you've come to base camp either on your own or with your partner, with an open mind and a willingness to do what it takes and support each other on the journey to the pinnacle.

The first stage (15%) of the journey is about **stretching your legs,** feeling out your fitness level at the start of a journey. It might lead to regretting the coffees and muffins you've eaten over the last few years, as you learn what did and didn't support you on this new adventure. This is about understanding your own money personality, beliefs, and the stories you have. It's also about understanding your emotions and how they impact your decision-making and what money means to you. You'll consider the similarities and differences with your partner. At this stage, you aren't ready to change anything yet, or even engage in the money conversation, but listening and observing helps you understand why you are where you are and how to prepare to take the next steps.

Getting into your stride. At this stage, you've started to climb the mountain and are finding your stride and your pace. About 1/3rd of the way up it's time for a pitstop to refuel. If you have been taking the journey on your own, it's quite possible that the stars align and you fall in love with someone. This is where you can either head back down to base camp for you to have a refresher and start the journey together or just relax and let your partner catch up by doing the individual work you have already done. You can take a bit of a breather and admire the view. With your partner by your side, you look at your money personalities and how they fit together. This is where a lot of couples get an '*aha*' moment—the light bulb flashes and they can see why they do what they do and why the other does what they do. Your money personality is just a behaviour style, so you can change it if it doesn't serve you or your relationship. Every personality has strengths and weaknesses. Knowing yours, you can put your strengths together with your partner's and push on to the next level of understanding.

Keep going... you've made it to **the half way point**. At this stage, you've done a lot of great work. You've learned how men and women handle finances differently. You respect those differences because paired with yours, they serve your relationship well. You also know when you need to step back and let the other be masculine or feminine. You know that healthy relationships will also have arguments and how to navigate hard conversations maturely. You might even be dipping your toes in the icy water and trying out a money conversation.

Check your oxygen mask. It's time for the last push to the summit. This can be frustrating as you just want to get to the top already, but there are some final checks before the final push. You don't want to "arrive" prematurely, cause an avalanche, and have everything come crashing down. One way to cause an avalanche at this stage is financial infidelity. This is one of the biggest breaches of trust a couple can have, and it can stop you from reaching the top. You might need to call in an expert to help you get over this boulder before you can move forward again.

You've made it! You are standing on **the pinnacle**. The view is amazing. It's crystal clear. You are standing together holding hands and taking deep breaths, savouring the moment. You have a clear understanding of each other's strengths and weaknesses when it comes to money. You don't need to keep secrets from each other because you have no problem talking about money. You make joint decisions and talk about creating wealth and long-term plans together. You understand that sometimes you will need to compromise and you are not concerned about having that conversation. You have regular financial date nights and you both know and understand where you are financially and where you are going.

As a result of this level of communication, there is a very strong commitment to your relationship and your family as a unit.

At the top of the mountain is a flag with these four statements which demonstrate a healthy relationship with money:

1. **We don't avoid money.** You know exactly what you owe and what you own. You check credit card and bank statements. You know what payments are coming up and when. This doesn't mean you always get it right, but if something unexpected happens, you don't bury your head in the sand; you are prepared and able to deal with it.

2. **We live within our means**. You know how much is coming in and how much is going out. You save for your holidays and other large purchases. You have a retirement plan in place and when the credit card bill arrives you pay the full amount. This doesn't mean you live a frugal lifestyle and never have fun with your money. You do! You have learnt how to make wise choices.

3. **We don't keep secrets from ourselves or each other**. You are open and honest with yourself about how much you spend. There aren't items hidden in the back of the wardrobe, or tucked away in the garage, that you've 'had for months' but in reality, you bought yesterday and just didn't want to disclose. The only things hidden away are the birthday gifts for your partner!

4. **We have examined our money beliefs and stories and aligned them with our values**. You have taken the time to understand why you have the relationship with money that you have. You've worked through your beliefs and your money stories separately, talked about them together, and established where they have come from and whether they are working for you or not. Those that work, you have kept, and those that don't, you have

moved on from. You have wrapped your values around your relationship and made them the focus of your decision-making.

It doesn't matter where you are on the mountain right now, the important thing is that you keep climbing. It's fine to stop to refresh and recharge yourself along the way, but then keep moving.

Gaz and I didn't even make it to base camp in our joint money journey!

After Gaz and I went our separate ways, I carried on with my life and business, being a complete ostrich about my financial situation until I had my public meltdown on a park bench with a client, which I shared in Chapter 4. After asking me what was wrong, the next question was 'Well, what are you going to do about it'? That stopped the tears.

'What?' I replied. 'There's nothing I can do about it'. Shame and fear had got me so stuck, I couldn't see a way out of the situation I was in.

'Of course there is', was the reply. Next thing I knew, the trusty notebook that I always carried was put to good use. There on that park bench, the list was written that started pulling me back from the brink.

On that list was a name: Simon. I had known Simon for several years. His name was on my list as he'd been asking me to do joint workshops with him. I knew this could bring new clients into my practice, but due to my state of mind, I kept resisting. But now it was on the to-do list. I reached out to Simon and over the course of doing the workshops together, our friendship blossomed into a relationship that lasted 13 years.

Simon was by my side as I made the tough decisions to get myself out of the mess I was in. He listened to me struggle with my university papers and writing essays. I recall saying to him one day, 'If I have to read another pigeon study, they are going into a pie'! He was also with me as I tested ideas and concepts for Money Mentalist, and for that and more I will be eternally grateful.

As I learned more, we would take tentative steps up the mountain together. I don't think we made it quite to the top, but we certainly made it a lot further than Gaz and I did. Simon and I weren't perfect in our communication about money, and I don't expect you to be either. It isn't easy. But if you don't try, where will you be a year from now? Five years? Twenty years? You have nothing to lose and everything to gain by trying.

Naturally, I didn't expect the call that day. I didn't recognize the number, but I picked it up anyway.

'Lynda', the familiar voice said. 'Gaz isn't well. In fact, he's in Hospice and isn't expected to be around for more than a week or so...'

At this point, we'd been separated for over 12 years. I couldn't even imagine him any way other than vibrant and full of life. I was speechless. The caller gave me Gaz's contact info if I wanted to reach out while there was time. I had no idea what to do. Would Gaz even want to see me?

My then-partner, Simon, had supported his wife as she battled and subsequently away from cancer, so he immediately understood the situation and was a huge support to me with his wise advice. His response was immediate: 'Call him and go see him'.

Those words were another catalyst for the book you're holding in your hand. I had no idea what Gaz was going through, or what the morphine was doing, but Simon did, as he had been through this with his wife. He so completely understood both aspects and was able to guide me about what was happening and what to expect over the next few weeks.

I took Simon's advice and began regularly driving 40 minutes in both directions to sit with Gaz in his final days. Those days unlocked everything you're holding in your hand.

It's amazing, isn't it, how life comes around in these full circle moments? How sometimes we catch a glimpse of how the pain we've endured can be repurposed for something incredible. It might be easy to regret the things Gaz and I hadn't known to save our relationship, but then the hundreds of people and relationships I've coached would still be floundering. For our one relationship, hundreds more have found the keys they need. And now with this book, even more people can take the keys and unlock a future I didn't get with Gaz.

Dear one, take hold of this moment. Don't let fear overtake you. Find what makes you brave and cling to it. This life is worth your full investment.

I'm here to help in any way I can.

WHAT NOW?

This book was created to develop your own money love story, remove financial blocks and creat more wealth in your life.

By challenging you to think about the following:

- Your relationship with money, and how it impacts your decisions
- Your money beliefs, and whether these are holding you back or helping you move forward
- What financial fulfilment means and looks like for you
- Setting short - and long-term goals that will start you on the road to success

Whether you are aware of it or not, the mindset and emotional relationship you have with money influences every spending decision that you make.

What's more, becoming financially fulfilled is actually 80% about understanding your relationship with money and your money beliefs. Only 20% is about practical money management.

If you have financial goals that you want to achieve, the single best thing you can do for yourself is understand your relationship with money – and change it for the better.

If you want to learn more: we have plenty of resources available on our website, sign up for our newsletter (https://moneymentalist.com/) and try our Money Personality quiz (https://money-mentalist.involve.me/whats-your-money-personality), or download our other ebooks, read our blogs, or simply ask us a question (https://moneymentalist.com/contact/).

Or, if you are ready to make some changes right now, then talk to me about **Fire Up Your Money Management Program.**

Hundreds of people have turned to me for help getting off the financial treadmill. I have life-changing programmes that will teach you how to reset your money mindset and change your habits so you can build a happy and successful life.

Fire-Up Your Money Management

If managing your money and paying off your mortgage faster or reaching new financial goals is your primary aim right now. This programme is for you.

The Fire-Up Your Money Management programme teaches you to manage your finances and bring awareness of your financial behaviour from the **back of your mind, to the front. You will learn how to successfully manage your money** with just 30 minutes a week.

I set you up with your own personalised online system, which I teach you how to use and monitor your progress. This system helps you track your spending, build your money plan and set your goals. I use behavioural economics to help you understand your income and expenses from a different perspective than usual accounting principles.

I check in on a regular basis to make sure you are staying on track. And each month we provide you with bonus resources to give you an insight and tips and tricks into your **financial behaviour and how you can improve.**

ACKNOWLEDGEMENTS

Mum and Dad – The best parents a girl could have. You have been there through all my ups and downs, and I am eternally grateful for your continued love and support no matter how crazy my life has been.

Amy – my amazing daughter. Even as a toddler you were very clear about what you wanted. That hasn't changed as you matured into the beautiful woman you are today. Thank you for always giving me a reason to spend money, from crockery as a three year old, to your Rotary Exchange to Argentina, we have so many fun stories to share and write about.. May you always have a loving relationship with money and learn from my journey.

Rose – Thank you for nurturing my desire to write a book and having the insight to interview me after Gaz's passing. You knew that one day they would become an integral part of my book.

Penny - Thank you for being my friend, PA, VA, Social media person, brainstorming buddy and every other role you have taken on to help me get to this point. And of course, for kicking my butt when I need it!

Marcy – I am so grateful for your amazing editing skills. I couldn't have completed this project without your help and sensitivity telling my story

My clients – Past and present and future. Working with you all has been inspiring, challenging at times, but always rewarding. My business wouldn't be where it is today without you all.

Gaz – You are the inspiration behind the book, you may not be with us anymore, but your spirit lives on in every page.

Lise – Thank you for your expertise and marketing skills which have enabled me to focus on what I needed to do and leave the rest in your capable hands.

David - Thank you for taking my call all those years ago when I was an accountant with a crazy idea to learn about money mindset. Your programme turned my life around, and going on to become a certified coach under your Mentorship has helped me help so many others

Sarah – Thanks for being my accountability buddy in the very early days of Money Mentalist. You encouraged me to keep going with the business idea when I wanted to give up as it was just too hard. Your ongoing support and friendship was invaluable to me when I was with Gaz in the hospice.

Taylor - Thank you for being my accountability coach. We talked about me writing a book right at the start or coaching relationship and now it has happened! Accountability really does work...

Ann – You have been in my life since our children were at primary school, we have both grown so much as mothers, business owners and friends. I love the time we spend together (often with a glass of Chardonnay) talking about business, life and our children.

Joy – We found each other at Gaz's beside when he was in hospice. Our love of music cemented our friendship, and your encouragement and piano lessons drew the creativity out of me which helped put the words onto paper too.

Simon – You picked up the pieces when I had hit rock bottom, helped me get through my university studies and the challenges of growing Money Mentalist. I never did need to make that pigeon pie!

My grandmother – 98 years young and still going strong. You are my inspiration that it is never too late to start something new.

This was one of the hardest parts of the book to write as there are so many other people who have crossed my path over the years who have shared their stories with me, listened to mine, and given me advice, every conversation had a gem in it and has helped me write the book. I thank you all.

ABOUT LYNDA MOORE

B.COM, GRAD DIP ARTS (PSYCH), FTA

I started my career as an accountant when I was 17. I love numbers, to me they tell a story of your business and your life. I read them like others read novels. I graduated from University with a B.Com. After working for several accounting firms, when I was 7 months pregnant with my daughter (now 33), I began my own practice. I remained in Public Practice until 2010 when I sold my business to return to university to study Psychology.

In the middle of all of this, my marriage ended. Anecdotally, 70-80% of relationships break up because of money and this was true in my situation. I was devastated, and an emotional wreck. Even though I was an accountant, which meant I had a sound knowledge of my own financial situation, that didn't really help me going through my own breakup. Emotions completely took over. I felt I was completely on my own. I came out the other side servicing $600,000 of debt.

It may seem a strange change in career path from accounting to Psychology, but it made complete sense to me. What I had realised in my years in practice, is that accounting (and money) isn't just about the numbers, it is also about the emotions that go behind the numbers, it's how we see the world and how we make decisions all stem from our relationship with money.

I graduated again this time with a Post Graduate Diploma in Arts (Psych). I continued to specialise in Money Psychology by continuing my training with Professor David Krueger (author of the Book 'The Secret Language of Money') and became a certified Money Mentor Coach.

What Changed?

- I learned the distinction between a budget and a money plan.
- I started saying No to myself and others about things that didn't really matter to me.

And saying Yes to what was important to me. This was when I really saw the impact of mindset on moving the numbers.

- I learned how to make the tough decisions that helped me turn my life around.
- I rewrote my own Money Story.

The Money Mentalist was born, and I now spend my time working with individuals and couples helping them understand their relationship with money, how to communicate about money to each other and how to make better financial choices. I use my accounting expertise to help them build a Money Plan (I don't use the term budget) which gives them the confidence to manage their money to reach their financial goals.

Contact:

- Email: lynda@moneymentalist.com
- Facebook: @moneymentalist
- Instagram: @lyndakmoore
- TikTok: @moneymentalist
- LinkedIn: lyndakmooremoneymentalist
- Web: www.moneymentalist.com

www.ingramcontent.com/pod-product-compliance
Lightning Source LLC
Chambersburg PA
CBHW051048050726
47592CB00002B/436